VIKING

THE ESSENTIALS OF HINDUISM

TRILOCHAN SASTRY is Professor at IIM Bangalore and a former Dean. He did his BTech from IIT Delhi, MBA from IIM Ahmedabad and PhD from MIT. He is the founder of ADR, an NGO that works on electoral and political reforms, and also of CCD and Farmveda, which works with tens of thousands of small farmers. Sastry has received various awards for his academic work and for his work in society. He has been interested in Hinduism since early adolescence and has lived in monasteries, studied the sacred texts, attended classes from various teachers and visited various pilgrimage sites.

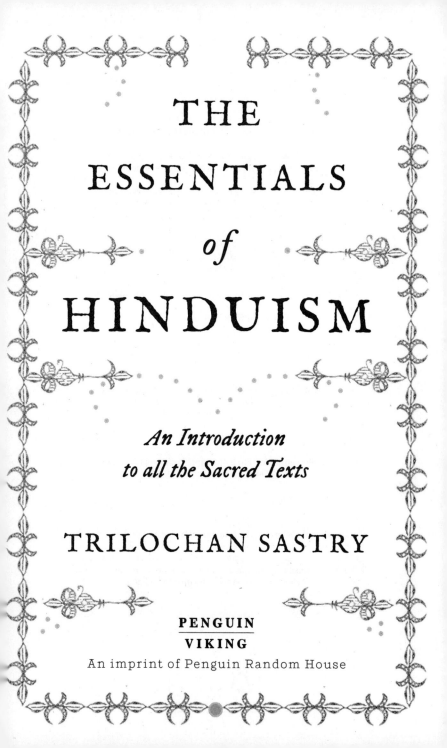

THE
ESSENTIALS
of
HINDUISM

*An Introduction
to all the Sacred Texts*

TRILOCHAN SASTRY

**PENGUIN
VIKING**

An imprint of Penguin Random House

VIKING

USA | Canada | UK | Ireland | Australia
New Zealand | India | South Africa | China | Singapore

Viking is part of the Penguin Random House group of companies
whose addresses can be found at global.penguinrandomhouse.com

Published by Penguin Random House India Pvt. Ltd
4th Floor, Capital Tower 1, MG Road,
Gurugram 122 002, Haryana, India

First published in Viking by Penguin Random House India 2022

Copyright © Trilochan Sastry 2022

All rights reserved

11 10 9 8

The views and opinions expressed in this book are the author's own and the
facts are as reported by him, which have been verified to the extent possible,
and the publishers are not in any way liable for the same.

ISBN 9780670096763

Typeset in Adobe Garamond Pro by Manipal Technologies Limited, Manipal
Printed at Thomson Press India Ltd, New Delhi

www.penguin.co.in

CONTENTS

PREFACE

This short introductory book is meant for those who have an interest in Hinduism but do not have the time or inclination to study all the texts. Unlike other great religions that are based on a small set of books, there are hundreds of texts in Hinduism, most of which are very voluminous. They span not merely centuries, but millennia. The ancient scriptures are all in Sanskrit, a language which many do not know. The beginner is sometimes bewildered and does not know where to start such a study. A short introductory text covering the entire range of scriptures may serve that purpose. It may be of special interest to lay interested readers from other religions and nations as well as those who are agnostic or atheistic.

The ancient word is Sanatana Dharma or the Eternal Religion. However, we will continue to use the word 'Hinduism' as it is widely used today. There is no founder and Hinduism says that the Eternal Truths have always existed. The early seers or *rishis* were the first to discover them.

The attempt is to present the scriptures as they are without any interpretation. Most of the available translations use the commentaries of later scholar-sages to interpret the earliest texts such as the Upanishads (which are a part of the Vedas), the Bhagavad Gita and the Brahma Sutras. They are the *prasthana traya* or foundational texts of Hinduism. For instance, it is rare to find a study of the Upanishads without the *bhashya* or commentary from one of the great commentators. The meaning of the original Upanishad is interpreted in the light of these *bhashyas*. This is true of all the Principal Upanishads, the Brahma Sutras and the Bhagavad Gita. Modern scholars have added to the variety of views on the scriptures. In this book, the original words of the scriptures are presented and several examples are given with a word-by-word translation. It is left to the reader to interpret it in his own way, and perhaps go back to other texts with more detailed explanations.

We present a brief overview of the Vedas, Upanishads, Brahma Sutras, the Six Darsanas or Philosophies, Bhagavad Gita, Puranas, Agama Sastras, other sacred scriptures such as the Vedangas, Upavedas, Smritis and other highly regarded texts, the great epics Ramayana and the Mahabharata, the medieval philosophies including Advaita, Visishtadvaita, Dvaita as well as the popular Bhakti movement which did not use Sanskrit. Such an overview of literature that spans millennia cannot be comprehensive. Inevitably, some kind of selection is required. Only the essential ideas are presented and the details are omitted. Interpretations based on history, politics and social conditions are entirely missing in this book. For discussions of these aspects, readers are referred to one of the many books available on such themes today.

To condense such a voluminous literature into a short text presents some challenges. What should be selected and what should be omitted? What aspects should be emphasized? The scriptures are open to various interpretations. The sacred texts that came later contain philosophies and commentaries based on the earlier Upanishads and Brahma Sutras and present different points of view. Even the texts themselves seem to have divergent views. For instance, the Puranas mention various gods such as Vishnu, Siva, Brahma, the Divine Mother and several others, whereas the Vedas do not mention most of them. Some texts emphasize reason and knowledge, and others emphasize devotion. The Vedas themselves seem to emphasize ritual in the earlier sections and knowledge in the later sections. On the surface, they all seem different. However, a deeper study shows an underlying harmony or consensus. The earliest attempt to find such a common ground is there in one of the foundational texts, the Brahma Sutras which contains the phrase तत्तु समन्वयात्, meaning 'but there is harmony'. It refers to the various Upanishads and says that there is harmony among them. For instance, the idea that each human being has a Soul, which in essence is Consciousness, is accepted by most schools of thought. Such essential ideas in the scriptures are given precedence in this book and presented as far as possible directly from the texts.

Where there are differences, all points of view are presented. For instance, the Six Philosophies or Shat Darsanas as well as the later Great Philosophies such as the Advaita, the Visishtadvaita and the Dvaita have differences. The essence of these philosophies is presented.

In addition to the original scriptures, there are many modern scholars who have written about the basic tenets of Hinduism. Modern-day sages such as Ramakrishna, Vivekananda, Ramana Maharshi, Aurobindo and many others have provided a fresh insight into these ancient scriptures. The ancient *maths* or monasteries of different philosophical persuasions as well as many modern monasteries and institutions have English publications and translations of the ancient scriptures. In today's digital age, many scriptures are available online. All these are also source materials for this introductory text. Whenever a point needed clarification, the original scripture was consulted.

In addition to Sanskrit, several Indian languages have texts that are often regarded as scriptures in that region. Hindi, Marathi, Bengali, Tamil, Kannada, Telugu and other Indian languages have many texts which are held in high regard and esteem. They are regarded as scripture in the respective regions. This book does not discuss them except in passing.

India has been the origin of other great religions. All of them did not use Sanskrit. The Buddhist scriptures were originally written in Pali. The Sikh religious book, Guru Granth Sahib uses several languages including Punjabi, Sanskrit and Persian. The original Jain teachings were in Ardhamagadhi, although later they were made available in various languages. In many ways, Buddhism, Jainism and Sikhism influenced the practice of Hinduism. However, in this book, we do not discuss the other great religions that originated in India. Another religious tradition which continues to the present day may be called 'folk religion'. These include both rural and tribal religions and practices. In their original form, they emerged from the people in diverse regions and had different rituals, beliefs and practices. However, all these streams have intermingled with Hinduism, each influencing the other. The focus of this book however will be on the Hindu scriptures.

Hinduism also includes rituals, festivals and different forms of worship. It mentions worship of literally thousands of gods and goddesses. These rituals vary from region to region and also change from time to time. They also change for the same individual as he goes through different phases of life. This book does not discuss rituals except in passing. It is widely accepted that although rituals vary, the goals they seek to eventually achieve are similar. These objectives which the rituals help to achieve are there in the texts, either as revelation or philosophy.

The sequence of chapters approximately follows the historical development of the scriptures. The Vedas and the earliest Upanishads are the most ancient and are also considered to be the most sacred. The book begins with them. The next two chapters deal with the Shat Darsanas or Six Philosophies which came a little later. The Brahma Sutras, which are perhaps the most important of these six, are in a separate chapter. This is followed by a brief chapter on the Bhagavad Gita. Since it is the most widely translated text, we discuss only the new ideas and teachings in the Gita. The three sacred texts—the Vedas, the Brahma Sutras and the Bhagavad Gita—are often referred to as the *prasthana traya* or the three foundational texts of Hinduism. Chapters on other sacred texts including the Puranas, Agama Sastras and the Itihasas or the Great Epics follow. There are other highly regarded texts including the Upavedas, Vedangas, Smritis, the various texts also using the suffix Gita, and a few spiritual texts derived from the Ramayana. All of them are discussed in a chapter entitled 'Other Sacred Texts'. The Puranas, Agama Sastras and texts using the suffix 'Smriti' developed over centuries, and it is not possible to say clearly which came earlier and which followed later. All these form part of the ancient scriptures.

In the medieval times, several great philosophical texts were written. They are discussed in the chapter entitled 'The Great Philosophies'. Of them, Advaita, Visishtadvaita and Dvaita are well known. All of them establish their philosophies citing the Upanishads and the Brahma Sutras as testimony. The devotional offshoots of the philosophies, such as Bhedabheda and Shudhadvaita, and the philosophical knowledge-based branches, such as *ajata vada*, *drishti-srishti* and *srishti-drishti*, are also discussed briefly. In the chapter entitled 'The Bhakti Tradition', there is a very brief description of more modern texts by medieval saints in local spoken languages unlike the ancient texts which were in Sanskrit. They were often in the form of songs and pithy sayings that resonated with the masses. We conclude with an attempt to present the essential ideas on which there is a consensus.

Approximate Timeline of the Scriptures

It is difficult to assign precise dates to the scriptures and there are several scholars who have proposed different dates. Many of the texts were orally recited and were put down in written form much later. This makes it more difficult to date them. However, what is known with certainty is that the Vedas are the most ancient. The latter portion of the Vedas are the Upanishads. After this, we have the Six Darsanas, including the Brahma Sutras. The Bhagavad Gita comes soon after and is a part of the Mahabharata. The Ramayana is widely believed to predate the Bhagavad Gita. The Smritis, Puranas and Agama Sastras also came after the Vedic period and all the texts, particularly the Puranas evolved over centuries. The bulk of the sacred texts were composed before the advent of Christianity.

Buddhism and Jainism, though not formally a part of the Hindu religion, most likely evolved after the Bhagavad Gita. Later Hindu texts refer to them.

Much later during the medieval period, beginning from around the 8th century CE, the Vedanta philosophies of Advaita, Visishtadvaita and Dvaita evolved together with the Shudhadvaita and Dvaitadvaita, variations of which are known as Bhedabheda Vada and Achintya Bhedabheda. The medieval period also saw the emergence of the Bhakti movement. This helped to spread religion to the masses as the sayings, texts and songs were in local languages.

Date	Scriptures					
1800 BCE	Vedas					
1700						
1600						
1500						
1400						
1300						
1200						
1100						
1000						
900						
800						
700	Major Upanishads					
600					Birth of	
500		Brahma Sutras, Sankhya	Ramayana		Gautama Buddha, Mahavira, Buddhism and Jainism	

Preface

Period						
400		Other darsanas	Bhagavad Gita and Mahabharata			
300						
200						
100		Manu Smriti and other major Smritis				
0						
100 CE						
200				Puranas		
300						
400						
500						
600	Minor Upanishads					
700			Advaita			Agama Sastras
800						
900						
1000			Visishtadvaita			
1100						
1200			Dvaita		The Bhakti Movement	
1300						
1400						
1500						
1600						
1700						
1800						
1900	Modern Sages—Ramakrishna, Vivekananda, Ramana Maharshi, Sri Aurobindo and others					
2000						

The questions addressed in this book include the following. What are the essential ideas and concepts in the Sanatana Dharma on which there is a wide consensus? Are there any scriptures that are considered more important than others? What is the significance of the Puranas which contain stories on various gods and goddesses, the origin of the universe and philosophy? Hinduism has the unique concept of the Divine Incarnation or *avatar* literally meaning the descent. This is taken to mean the descent of God on earth. What is this concept of the *avatar*? What, in essence, do the different systems of philosophy say? What is the ultimate benefit to be obtained by studying the scriptures or by following its teachings? Is there a harmony between the various Hindu scriptures which often differ amongst themselves?

If this helps anyone to get a basic understanding of various aspects of Hinduism and provides a basis for further study from more detailed texts, the book would have served its purpose.

1

THE VEDAS

In the Hindu scriptures, the highest position is accorded to the Vedas. The Vedas include the Upanishads, also known as Vedanta. Together, they are called the Shruti—that which is heard. The Vedas are the most ancient and are very voluminous. The belief is that the Vedic *rishis* or seers perceived something directly through revelation and chanted them as the Vedas.[1] In ancient times, the Vedas were not written down but were orally transmitted from one generation to the next. One interpretation of the term '*shruti*' is 'that which was heard', usually from the *guru* or teacher. Some others interpret '*shruti*' to mean 'that which was heard in revelation in moments of inspiration'. They are 'revealed texts', much like the Bible, Quran and the Sutta Pitaka of Buddhism. In other words, these texts were said to be revealed by God or a Higher Source in vision, voice or intuition.

Most later texts, scriptures and commentaries as well as sages and prophets in Hinduism have accepted the final authority of the Vedas. The Brahma Sutras, Bhagavad Gita, Smritis, Puranas, Shat Darsanas (Six Philosophies), Agama Sastras and Itihasas came later. All of them accept the authority of the Vedas. Every philosophy that came later tried to prove the truths of its assertions by using the authority of the Vedas. Although the Brahma Sutras and later philosophies such as the Advaita, Visishtadvaita and Dvaita differ from each other, they quote the Vedas—in particular, the Upanishads—as authority. The term 'sabda' or 'Veda pramana' is often used and means 'proof based on the Vedas'. The Gita also accepts the authority of the Vedas.[2] Modern-day scholar-saints like Vivekananda have observed, 'The only point where, perhaps, all our sects agree is that we all believe in the scriptures—the Vedas . . . Whatever be his philosophy or sect, everyone in India has to find his authority in the Upanishads . . . And the law is that wherever these Puranas and Smritis differ from any part of the Shruti, the Shruti must be followed and the Smriti rejected.'[3] Even today, all over India, scholars, *gurus*, temples, monasteries and sages accept the final authority of the Vedas.

The word 'Veda' is derived from the Sanskrit root word '*vid*'—to know. Veda simply means knowledge. The Sanskrit hymns are considered to be revelations of seers or *rishis*. It is believed that the Vedas are '*anaadi*' or without a beginning. A few centuries later, the well-known *rishi* Veda Vyasa classified them, perhaps for ease of study. They were organized and compiled* into four Vedas—the Rig, Yajur, Sama and Atharva. The Yajur Veda has two versions—the Krishna Yajur Veda taught by Vaishampayana and the Shukla Yajur Veda revealed to Yajnavalkya. Tradition says that these sages and their disciples and descendants kept their respective Veda alive by faithful chanting and by following its instructions.

The Rig Veda Samhita as available today has 1028 hymns or *suktas* in about 10,600 verses called Rk. arranged in twenty-one sections, the Yajur Veda has 1875 verses, the Sama Veda also has 1875 verses and the Atharva Veda has 6000 verses. In all, the Veda Samhitas have about 20,000 distinct *mantras* in ancient Sanskrit. Some of the hymns are found in more than one Veda. When we speak of Vedic chanting—sometimes called Veda *adhyayana* (literally, 'study') or Veda *parayana* (recitation)—we usually mean the Samhitas. The other verses in the Vedas, in the sections known as Brahmanas, Aranyakas and Vedanta or Upanishads, are in addition to the Samhitas.[4] It is believed that only a portion of the original Vedas are available today.

Let us first get a feel for what the Vedas are. They are meant to be chanted and both the chanter and listeners are usually required to understand the meaning of the

---

* One of the meanings of 'Vyasa' is to split or differentiate.

recitations. Reading about them is generally not considered enough. There is another school of thought which says that listening to the chanting is beneficial. Many so inclined today attest to the fact that listening calms the body and elevates the mind.[5] Ideally, we should listen to the Vedic chanting to imbibe the spirit of it. Today, many such renderings are available on the Internet. Before reading further, it is perhaps a good idea to listen for some time to these chants. There is a common belief that Vedic chanting done in the proper way provides many benefits, both temporal and spiritual.

The Vedas refer repeatedly to *devas*, literally 'bright ones', usually translated today as 'deities'. These are not the One Supreme God but manifestations of different aspects of it. Perhaps the idea is to manifest these *devas*, which becomes an aid to further religious or spiritual progress. For instance, the first *shloka* or verse of the Rig Veda is dedicated to Agni, the God who presides over Fire.

अग्निमीळे पुरोहितं यज्ञस्य देवं ऋत्विजं |
होतारं रत्नधातमम् ||

Agnimile purohitam, yajnasya devamrtvijam
hotaram ratnadhatamam

In some parts of the country, the first word is written and pronounced as '*Agnimide*'. To give a feel for the text we give as literal a translation as possible. What is given is one among the many popular English translations available.

> O Agni, I adore Thee,
> O priest, O divine minister
> Who officiates at the divine Sacrifice,
> Who is also the invoker, the Summoner,
> Who bestows the supreme divine wealth upon us.

- अग्नि—the deity Agni; ईळे—venerate, implore, extol; पुरोहितम्—priest; यज्ञस्य—of the sacrifice; ऋत्विजम्—priest (accusative singular)
- होतारम्—priest who invokes the deity or God
- रत्नधातमम्—superlative of 'bestower of treasure/wealth'; रत्न+धाता, referring to Agni.

However, we can get a sense of the difficulty if we probe a little.

पुरोहितः - पुरः धीयते असौ - One who is placed in front during Agni rituals
ऋत्विक् - ऋतौ यजति - One who performs Agni rituals at proper season/regularly
होता - जुहोति इति - One who offers oblations in Agni rituals

These three terms are used in the same verse and have almost the same meaning today. Other terms used in the Vedas

5

include 'Brahma' or 'Brahman', 'Adhvaryu' and 'Udgatri'. Their roots are different. Today, the word '*purohit*' is used most commonly, but the others are not that common.

Who is Agni? At one level, he is the God of Fire who is invoked in some Vedic rituals by lighting a fire and pouring oblations into it as the *mantras* are chanted. Others have interpreted Agni as the outer symbol of the inner light in us, which rituals help us to get in touch with or awaken. Some others like Sri Aurobindo have interpreted Agni as the Divine God of Will which we seek to manifest in ourselves. Modern scholars usually ignore the inner aspect and hold that Agni is the God of Fire. According to this view, in ancient times, man was drawn to worshipping different powers of nature. The word '*ratnadhatamam*', literally means the best (*uttamam*) among the givers or bestowers (*dhat*) of gems or jewels (*ratna*). Thus, Agni is the supreme bestower of jewels. Some have interpreted wealth not as mere jewellery but prosperity in all its dimensions, and others as divine wealth. This example illustrates the difficulty in translating and interpreting ancient Sanskrit in modern terms. Scholars have pointed out the differences between the ancient Vedic Sanskrit and the classical Sanskrit written by later poets such as Kalidasa and scholars like Adi Sankara. Given that there are over 20,000 *mantras* in the first Samhita part of the Vedas alone, there are bound to be differences in interpretations. We need to have a word-by-word understanding together with a sense of the meaning.

Some teachers say that whatever meaning appeals to a sincere student is the right meaning for that person. Perhaps it resonates with the inner nature of that person and so helps them in their religious or spiritual life.

History

There is no accepted date on which the Vedas were composed. Later, we shall see what the orthodox view on this issue is. However, if we go by the commonly accepted way of understanding history, we need to try and fix dates. There are references to several sages in the texts. Such a voluminous collection could only have been compiled over a long period of time.

Various scholars have suggested different dates of composition. One commonly accepted date of composition of the Rig Veda, is around 1800 BCE. However, there are others who have proposed a date as far back as 6000 BCE. Since for a long time the Vedas were not written down but transmitted from teacher to student, memorized and orally chanted, it is difficult to say when they were first composed. The orthodox view is that the Vedas should not be dated but are eternal and without beginning. We shall see how this is explained a little later.

The Essential Ideas Regarding the Vedas

There are some important ideas about the Vedas. These are from a slightly later philosophy or *darsana*. The Purva Mimamsa says that the Vedas are '*apaurusheya*' or 'not from man', that is, they are not composed by a human being. They are *anaadi* or without beginning, and limitless (*ananta*). They are also called the breath of God. Some scholars do not accept the concept of *apaurusheya* and quote Vedic texts as evidence. However, the most widely-accepted view is that they are indeed *apaurusheya*.

There are names of many *rishis* in the Vedas. Did they compose the hymns in which their names appear? For instance, the well-known Gayatri Mantra was composed by the sage Viswamitra. Then how can the Vedas be *apaurusheya*?[26] How can they be *anaadi*? The modern way of explaining this is to ask: did Isaac Newton discover gravity or did he invent it? Just as gravity has always existed, in the same way, the knowledge in the Vedas has always existed. The knowledge in the Gayatri Mantra—or, for that matter, in any other *mantra* or hymn has always existed. That knowledge is infinite. A part of this knowledge was revealed to the *rishis* and has come down as the Vedas. But the knowledge itself did not arise from a human source. In this sense, the Vedas are *apaurusheya* and *anaadi*. In fact, the 'authors' of many of the hymns are unknown. They are *ananta* or limitless because there is no limit to knowledge.

Although the Purva Mimamsa accepts this as true of all knowledge, it adds that the Vedas are faultless and need no revision. Not all later texts explicitly say this about the Vedas, but none have refuted them either. All texts accept their authority.

Going back to the meaning of the term 'Veda'—knowledge—it is up to us to interpret whether this refers only to that which is included in the Vedic texts or whether it also refers to the limitless knowledge that is constantly unfolding in science and other fields. The Vedas themselves refer to a vast number of verses that are no longer available with us today. The Vedas say that merely knowing the texts by rote will not lead anyone to the ultimate purpose of life. They even go on to say that belief in the Vedas is not essential for human life. Vivekananda observed, 'Of all the scriptures of the world, it is the Vedas alone which declare that the study of the Vedas is secondary.'[7] The Vedas are very liberal in this sense. Liberal in philosophy but orthodox in practice. In modern times, spiritual teachers say that following the teachings is more important than merely reading about them or grasping them intellectually.

The Vedas are also said to be the breath of God.[8] The question arises whether God created the Vedas. If He did, then there is a time before which the Vedas did not exist. But if they are *anaadi* or without beginning, this is not possible. So God and the Vedas have always existed. To reconcile this, the Vedas say that they are the breath of

God. They also give a simile that God and the Vedas are as closely connected as we are to our breath. The Vedas do not insist that there is only one way of leading a good life. Instead they say that any path followed with sincerity will lead to the same goal. The real method is 'that by which we realize the Unchangeable. And that is neither reading, nor believing, nor reasoning, but superconscious perception, or Samadhi'.[10]

Some Historical Preliminaries

The Vedas predate idol worship as we see in Hinduism today. There are many Vedic *devas,* literally 'shining' or 'bright ones' or 'deities' including Agni, Indra, the Ashvins, the Maruts, Rbhus, Rudra, Vayu, Brihaspati, Vishnu, Usha (Goddess of Dawn), the twin-deity Mitra–Varuna and Sarasvati (ancient Goddess of Learning). Some hymns are for all the gods—'*Viswedeva*'.

Worship done in the proper way invokes these deities. However, idol worship is entirely absent. There were no temples dedicated to these Vedic deities in ancient times, and there are none today. The gods that are popular today came much later, perhaps in the Puranic Age. There are some references to Matsya (Fish), Kurma (Tortoise) and Varaha (Boar) in the Vedas. Later, in the Puranic Age, they were incorporated into the list of *avatar* or Incarnations of God. Hinduism as practiced today is different from what it was in ancient times. However, it is based on the Vedas.

The Organization of the Vedas

The Vedas are broadly classified into four parts. The first part of each Veda is the Samhita, which contains hymns that are prayers and invocations to various Vedic deities like Indra, Agni, Vayu and so on. The second part, known as Brahmanas, explains the meaning of the hymns and rituals in the Samhita and gives injunctions on how the rituals are to be conducted. The third part is known as the Aranyakas and gives the symbolic and philosophical meanings of the hymns. The last part is known as the Vedanta or the Upanishads. They completely do away with rituals and gods and plunge straight into an exploration of the nature of Ultimate Reality and how we as human beings can reach the goal of life. The first two parts of the Vedas are also known as the Karma Kanda (the *karma* or ritual portion). The word '*karma*' has at least three meanings. Here it refers to the Vedic rituals as *karma*. The phrase 'Vedic *karma*' is still in use. In later texts such as the Gita, *karma* also refers to action and the law of cause and effect. Sometimes, it also refers to the sum total of all actions done by an individual as his or her *karma*. The latter two portions of the Vedas are referred to as the Jnana Kanda or the Way of Knowledge. However, this classification is not watertight since there are profound philosophical verses in the Karma Kanda and ritualistic verses in the Jnana Kanda.

The Rig Veda is the most voluminous. Many consider it to be the first of the Vedas. However, there are references to other Vedas in the Rig Veda, and so it becomes difficult to establish this. All its verses are in the form known as Rk or Rik. They are also known as *shlokas* or stanzas. Since it begins with a hymn to Agni, sometimes it is popularly understood to promote fire worship. However, many interpret 'Agni' to be the light of one's soul or consciousness.

The famous Gayatri Mantra is from this Veda, though it is also found in the Yajur and Sama Vedas. It also has the well-known Nasadiya Suktam, popularly known as the Hymn of Creation. The Purusha Suktam, chanted even today, is from this Veda, although it also occurs in the Yajur and Atharva Vedas with some slight differences. The Rig Veda also has marriage rites drawn from the marriage of Surya's (Sun God) daughter. There are highly poetic compositions dedicated to Usha, the Goddess of Dawn.

In addition to the 10,600 verses in the Samhita, the Rig Veda has the Aitareya, Kausitaki and Sankhayana Brahmanas, and the Aitareya and Sankhayana Aranyakas. One of the Principal Upanishads as classified much later by Adi Sankaracharya, namely the Aitareya Upanishad is from the Rig Veda. The Rig Veda contains other Upanishads as well.

The Yajur Veda comes from the root '*yaj*' meaning 'worship'. The word '*yajna*' or 'sacrifice' is also derived from it. The Yajur Veda has two versions—the Krishna and Shukla Yajur Vedas. 'Krishna' here means 'dark' and 'Shukla' means 'white'.[11] The Yajur Veda has a very large section on ritual Vedic worship and its inner meaning. This is largely written in prose and not in the poetical Rk form of the Rig Veda. However, it has many *mantras* that are sacred. It also has Rk *mantras*, some from the Rig Veda and others not found in it. The original Yajur Veda was taught by Vaishampayana to Yajnavalkya. Due to a misunderstanding, the disciple had to return the Veda to his *guru*. Yajnavalkya later invoked the Sun God and got knowledge again. This became known as the Shukla (white) Yajur Veda. The earlier version taught by Vaishampayana became known as the Krishna (black) Yajur Veda.

The Shukla Yajur Veda has two major Brahmanas— the Vajasaneyi Brahmana and the Shatapatha Brahmana (literally, 'one with a hundred chapters') and is very lengthy. There is another recension (or scholarly revision of a text or scripture) called the Kanva Shakha, which some scholars say is more ancient and has 104 chapters. It deals mainly with Vedic rituals and worship. The Krishna Yajur Veda has the Taittiriya Brahmana and provides complete descriptions of Vedic rituals, including the Rajasuya and Ashvamedha *yajnas* or sacrifices which are performed by kings. These sacrifices were performed in later times as described in both the Ramayana and the Mahabharata.

Some of the well-known *shlokas* chanted today, including the Rudram, are from the Yajur Veda. Today the Shukla Yajur Veda is prevalent mostly in north India and the Krishna Yajur Veda primarily in south India.

Like the other Vedas, both the Yajur Vedas have several Upanishads in the concluding portions. Among the ten Principal Upanishads as classified later by Adi Sankara, the Shukla Yajur Veda has the Isa and Brihadaranyaka Upanishads. The Krishna Yajur Veda has the Katha and Taittiriya Upanishads. The Krishna Yajur Veda also contains the Svetaswatara Upanishad, another important Upanishad.

The Sama Veda ('*sama*' means 'that which brings peace' or '*shanti*') is said to bring happiness through peace of mind. Many of the Rig Vedic hymns are set to music in the Sama Veda. It is chanted in a musical way and is said to be the origin of Indian music. It largely has Rks, most of them from the Rig Veda and additional ones as well. In the Bhagavad Gita, Lord Krishna highly extols the Sama Veda and says, 'Among the Vedas, I am Sama Veda.' The Divine Mother Lalita is also '*samaganapriya*' or 'One who is pleased by the recital of the Sama Veda'. The Sama Veda has the Kena and Chandogya Upanishads, two of the principal Upanishads.

'*Atharva*' means 'priest' or 'wise man'. Atharva Rishi is mentioned in the Veda. It has many *mantras* for warding off evil and hardship and destroying enemies. The contents are in prose as well as in verse. There are verses dedicated to *devas* who are not mentioned in the other Vedas. It has verses dealing with creation, such as the Prithvi Suktam, evocative of the Nasadiya Suktam in the Rig Veda. Among the Principal Upanishads, the Prasna, Mundaka and Mandukya are found in the Atharva Veda. It does not have any Aranyaka, but has the Gopatha Brahmana.

Samhita

The first portion of the Vedas is called the 'Samhita'. This literally means 'putting together'. More formally, it refers to hymns (or *suktas*) in specific poetic meters and arranged according to some rules.* The hymns are said to be revelations of various sages or *rishis*. Each hymn consists of a set of *mantras*. The literal meaning of the word 'mantra' is 'that which protects the mind'—*manah* (or *mananat*) *trayate, iti mantra*. By repetition and dwelling on its meaning, the *mantra* protects the mind. *Mantras* are also said to purify the mind. They are considered potent and said to have the power to confer temporal and spiritual benefits to those who chant them in the proper way.

To get a feel for the spirit of the Samhitas, some of the famous hymns are described. The spirit can only be

---

* Many languages have poetic metres prescribing the number of syllables per line, the number of lines per stanza, and so on. Metre serves to give poetry a rhythmical and sometimes melodious sound.

captured by hearing the hymns chanted in the proper way in their entirety. One famous hymn is the Gayatri Mantra which was first revealed to the sage Viswamitra and is given in the Samhita of the Rig Veda. It also appears in the Yajur Veda and the Sama Veda. The opening phrase is as follows:

ॐ भूर्भुवस्वः| or *Om Bhūr Bhuva-Swah'* is an invocation.

The *mantra* has three lines of eight syllables each. This is now called the Gayatri metre and several other verses in the Rig Veda are composed in this metre.

ॐ भूर्भुवस्वः । तत्सवितुर्वरेण्यम् । भर्गो देवस्य धीमहि । धियो यो नः प्रचोदयात्

Om Bhūr Bhuva-Swah', Tat savitur varenyam, Bhargo devasya dhīmahi, Dhiyo yo nah prachodayāt
                                           —Rig Veda 3.62.10;
                          Yajur Veda, Chapter 36, *Mantra* (Verse) 3;
                                           Sama Veda: 2.812

A word-by-word translation without interpretation is as follows:[12]

tat–that (God); *savitur*–of the sun; *varenyam*–the best; *bhargo* (*bhargas*)–light, illumination; *devasya*–divine; *dhimahi*–let us meditate; *dhiyo* (*dhiyah*)–intelligence; *yo* (*yah*)–which; *nah*–our; *prachodayat*–may it push, inspire, illumine

16

The invocation 'Om a sacred syllable indicating the Highest reality *bhur-bhuva-swah*' denotes the earth, sky and space. It invokes in a sense the Highest Reality as the earth, sky and space.

There are many free translations which strive to convey the meaning in English. One such translation is:

That Sun (we) adore, on whose Supreme effulgence (we) meditate. May that Light illumine our intellect (or us).

This famous *mantra*, discovered by Viswamitra is considered to be very powerful and purifies those who practice or repeat it daily with sincerity. It can also lead to the highest goal of life—to illumination. The 'Sun' here does not refer to the physical sun. It is a symbol of light, denoting the Highest on which we meditate.

Another famous *mantra* often quoted from the Samhita is:

एकं सद्विप्रा बहुधा वदन्ति

Ekam Sat, Vipra Bahudavadanti

This can be translated as: 'The Truth is One, the wise call it by various names.' It indicates that though there are a multitude of gods and deities like Agni, Indra and so on, they all refer to One God or Reality. In Vedic times, the later religions did not exist. In the spirit of this Vedic *shloka* or verse, all concepts of God come from that One Truth which sages of different religions called by different names. In modern times, Sri Ramakrishna, a 19th-century sage, said 'The Hindus call it *jal*, the Christians call it water, and Muslims call it *paani*. It refers to the same substance.'[13] In this sense, this Vedic *mantra* says that there is only One Truth and sages call it by various names.

Another oft-quoted *mantra* is:

आ नो भद्राः क्रतवो यन्तु विश्वतः

Aa no bhadrah kratvo yantu visvatah

[Let noble thoughts come to us from every side]
—Rig Veda, 1-89

Another famous set of *mantras* is the Purusha Suktam in hymn 10.90 of the Rig Veda. It is found in the Shukla Yajur Veda Samhita 30.1-16, the Krishna Yajur Veda Aranyaka 3.12.1-18, an abridged version in the Sama Veda and in the Atharva Veda Samhita 19.6. This hymn is recited regularly during various religious events even today. It is an invocation of the Purusha, the Supreme Self. It refers to the Supreme Purusha in the opening *mantra* as One with a thousand heads, a thousand eyes and a thousand feet, pervading the entire universe and extending even beyond it. Already, we can see the concept of an all-pervading Reality which is in the universe as Immanent and beyond

it as Transcendent. Some other inspiring verses in the
Purusha Suktam include:

वेदाहमेतं पुरुषं महान्तम् |
आदित्यवर्णंतमसःपरस्तात् |
तमेवं विद्वानमृतं इह भंवति |

Vedahametam Purusha mahantam, aditya varnam
tamasa parastaat.
Tam eva vidvan, amrutam iha bhavati

[I have known that Supreme *Purusha*, brilliant like the
Sun, beyond all darkness. By knowing Thou (Purusha)
alone, Immortality is attained even here.]

We see here one of the essential ideas in Hinduism. Not
only is there an Ultimate reality, but I too can experience
it. Its nature as partly explained here—it is brilliant like the
Sun and beyond all darkness. Sages have said that it is not
the physical light that is referred to here. Later, we shall
see that the idea of 'light' to indicate illumination is used
again and again in various scriptures, including some non-
Hindu ones. The idea that there is some ultimate heaven
or redemption for which we have to wait after death is also
missing. It says that Immortality is here and now.

The Hymn of Creation, called the Nasadiya Suktam, is
another profound set of *mantras*. It is found in the Rig Veda

Samhita (10:129). It is about the process of Creation itself and starts off with the following verses, freely translated into English, and shows the spirit of enquiry about the Origin of the Universe. Whether this is mere speculation, imagination, inspiration or some kind of revelation is a matter of individual interpretation. The *mantra* begins with the following verses:

Existence was not then, nor non-existence;
The world was not, the sky beyond was neither.
What covered the mist? Of whom was that?
What was in the depths of darkness thick?

Death was not then, nor immortality;
The night was neither separate from day,
But motionless did *That* vibrate
Alone, with Its own glory one—
Beyond *That*, nothing did exist.

In popular writings, this is sometimes compared to the Big Bang Theory of modern physics where the universe as we know it is believed to have originated from an infinitesimally high-density 'substance' followed by a big bang that, over millions of years, evolved into the sun, earth, planets and galaxies that we now see.[14]

Apart from metaphysical poetry, there are hymns regarding marriage and death as well. The Samhitas in general are invocatory *mantras*. A group of *mantras* comprise a '*sukta*' or hymn. The Rig Veda Samhita has ten '*mandalas*' or groups.

There are hymns for the marriage rituals, as well as for death. The very last mantra of the last (10th) Mandala of the Rig Veda Samhita is also well known. The last verse of the *mantra* is:

समानेन वो हविषा जुहोमि ||
समानी व आकूति: समाना हृदयानि व:|
समानमस्तु वो मनो यथा व: सुसहासति ||

samānena vo haviṣā juhomi ||
samanī va ākūtiḥ samānā hrdayāni vaḥ |
samānamastu vo mano yathā vaḥ susahāsati ||

The spirit of this last hymn of the Rig Veda is that we should all work together, walk together and be of one purpose, mind and heart. It probably refers to the relationship between student and teacher, but can be applied to all common endeavours as well.

Similar hymns or *suktas* are there in the Samhita portion of the other Vedas. The Samhitas are said to be prayers to various gods or deities. They please the gods, purify the worshipper and also provide various benefits. It is said that the worship can yield worldly benefits like health, wealth, progeny and so on. However, if the fruits of worship are offered to the deity or to God (often by using the words '*na mama*,' meaning 'not for me'), then it purifies the worshipper and makes him ready for treading the path of liberation. Many of the prayers, especially those without a selfish motive, are not only for one's own benefit or spiritual purification but also for the good of society, the world and even the animals, plants and birds.

There are the '*shanti mantras*' or 'peace *mantras*' in the Vedas as well as the Vedanta. They are recited even today. They begin with the sacred syllable 'Om' and end with the invocation for peace: '*Om shanti, shanti, shanti.*' A few of the well-known ones are given below:

ॐ द्यौः शान्तिरन्तरिक्षं शान्तिः
पृथिवी शान्तिरापः शान्तिरोषधयः शान्तिः |
वनस्पतयः शान्तिर्विश्वेदेवाः शान्तिर्ब्रह्म शान्तिः
सर्वं शान्तिः शान्तिरेव शान्तिः सा मा शान्तिरेधि ||
ॐ शान्तिः शान्तिः शान्तिः ||

—यजुर्वेद ३६:१७

Oṃ dyauḥ śāntir antarikṣaṃ śāntiḥ
pṛthivī śāntir āpaḥ śāntir oṣadhayaḥ śāntiḥ
vanaspatayaḥ śāntir viśvedevāḥ śāntir brahma śāntiḥ
sarvaṃ śāntiḥ śāntir eva śāntiḥ sā mā śāntir edhi
oṃ śāntiḥ śāntiḥ śāntiḥ

—Yajur Veda 36:17

This is a famous *mantra* from the Yajur Veda and says:

> Om. May peace radiate there in the whole sky as well as in the vast ethereal space everywhere.
> May peace reign all over this earth, in water and in all herbs, trees and creepers.
> May peace flow over the whole universe.
> May peace be in the Whole Universe.
> And may there always exist in all peace and peace alone.
> Om peace, peace and peace to us and all beings!
>
> —Translation by Swami Abhedananda,
> Ramakrishna Vedanta Math

The prayer seeks peace everywhere—in matter, in trees and in all living beings.

Other examples include prayers such as '*Loka samastha sukhino bhavantu*' ('May the whole world be happy') and '*Sarve jana sukhino bhavantu*' ('May all beings be happy'). The Upanishads discussed in the next chapter also begin with *shanti mantras*.

From this very brief discussion, we can see that the classification of the Samhita as hymns aiding rituals that confer only 'worldly benefits' is not watertight since many of the hymns also contain deep philosophy.

Brahmana and Aranyaka

Veda Vyasa classified the second portion of each Veda as Brahmana. Here, it does not refer to any caste, gender or the Supreme Brahman, a word used repeatedly in the later Upanishads. There are no clear definitions of what this section is. Sayana, one of the earliest commentators on the Vedas, says that which is not a *sukta* or a *mantra* in tradition is Brahmana. Brahmanas contain explanations of various rituals, also called '*yajnas*' in the Vedas. Apastamba, another ancient scholar who lived probably in the first millennium bce, defined it as '*Karmacodana Brahmanani*', a phrase which means that the description of the '*karmas*' or rituals are in Brahmanas. They contain rules for the performance of rituals and the meaning of *mantras* and particular rites. Even today, the Vedic rituals are conducted according to these rules.

The word 'Aranyaka' is derived from '*aranya*' or forest and means 'from the forest'. This portion of the Vedas explains the inner meaning of the rituals described in the Brahmanas.

Upanishads

Literally, 'Upanishad' means 'to sit down near'. It is to sit down near a sage and gain the ultimate knowledge. The Upanishads come towards the end of the Aranyakas. Collectively, they are also known as 'Vedanta', meaning 'the end or goal of the Vedas'. Vedanta is now well-known not only in India but around the world. Since they form an important part of the Vedas, they are discussed in greater detail later.

Fitness for Learning the Vedas

There is one *shloka* or verse pertaining to those who are fit to learn the Vedas. The Sukla Yajur Veda (26.2) says:

यथेमां वाचं कल्याणीमावदानि जनेभ्यःब्रह्मराजन्याभ्यां शूद्राय चार्याय च स्वाय चारणाय ॥

Yathema vacham kalyanima vadani janebhya, brahma, raja, anyabhyam, sudraya charyaya cha svaya charanaya

[May I speak the Sacred Word to the masses of the people (*janebhya*), to the brahmana, the *kshatriya*, the *sudra* and the *arya*, and to our own men and the strangers. This includes all people.]

Later texts, including the Manu Smriti, have sometimes restricted the spread of Vedic learning to some sections of society. However, as some scholars including Vivekananda have pointed out, this goes against the words of the Vedas which say that everyone who is interested is fit to learn the Vedas.

Summary

The Vedas are the most ancient of the Hindu scriptures and are perhaps some of the oldest (if not *the* oldest) religious writings in the world. All the later sacred texts accept the Vedas as supreme, which include the Upanishads which are at the end of the Vedas. Collectively, they are called the Shruti or the 'revealed scriptures'. It is believed that the Vedas were revealed to the sages known as *rishis*, but not composed by them. Therefore, they are *apaurusheya* or 'not from man' and are also said to be eternal and infinite. A religious or spiritual interpretation would say that these Divine Truths always existed and were merely revealed to the *rishis* in higher states of consciousness. A modern scientific view would be very similar, saying that knowledge has always existed and that the *rishis* (or modern-day scientists) merely discovered that knowledge.

The Hindu religion is also said to be the Vedic religion because all later texts, including the famous Bhagavad Gita, accept the supremacy of the Vedas. Whenever there is a difference between any text and the Vedas or Upanishads, the latter are accepted as true.

2

UPANISHADS OR VEDANTA

The Upanishads declare that each soul is potentially divine. This can be realized here and now, in this very life. It is variously called 'Brahman', 'Atman' or 'Purusha' and is within us. Knowledge of or realization of this Truth makes us free of all sorrow, and gives everlasting bliss or joy. It transform us completely. In the Sanatana Dharma, the Upanishads are regarded as the highest. All later scriptures have to conform to the Upanishads.

The Upanishads contain revelations about the nature of Ultimate Reality. They are revealed texts much as other religions consider that God revealed knowledge to various prophets. They are found in the last part of the Vedas. They are also called Vedanta, meaning 'the end or final goal of the Vedas'. They are included in the term '*shruti*' (literally, 'that which was heard') used for the highest scriptures. This is in contrast to the later scriptures called Smritis ('that which was remembered'). There are several interpretations of the term '*shruti*'. One is that in ancient times, the Vedas were chanted and memorized and thus were only heard. Hence, they are called Shruti. Another interpretation is that '*shruti*' refers to that which was heard by the *rishis* in revelation. Closely related to this is the idea of '*mantra drashta*'—the seer of the *mantra*.[1] We discuss the idea of *mantra* in detail later, but they include the sacred verses we read in the Vedas (which includes the Upanishads). Whether the *mantras* are heard or seen in the physical sense is not relevant. They are revealed to the seers or *rishis* in a higher state of consciousness. That knowledge always existed. The revelations are about the nature of the Ultimate Reality and man's relation to it. They also offer some guidelines for those seeking such direct knowledge. The Upanishads also clearly state that this revelation is available to anyone who is sincerely interested and is not limited only to the ancient *rishis*.

The Upanishads occupy a very important position in Hinduism. They are not mere philosophies with definitions, classifications of knowledge and explanations. They are not memories of teachings as given in the later texts known as Smritis. Such philosophies and descriptions came later. Each of the later philosophies uses the Upanishads as the basis for expounding their tenets. The Vedas, and in particular the Upanishads, are a litmus test to determine whether any philosophy fully aligns with them. The Six Darsanas or Philosophies and various other philosophies establish their point of view using the Upanishads. Even the Bhagavad Gita accepts the Upanishads and some of its verses are almost identical to Upanishadic verses. Centuries later, Adi Sankara, Ramanujacharya and Madhavacharya propounded different philosophies. Each quoted from the Upanishads to uphold their point of view.

The Upanishads are almost completely devoid of rituals and worship of any *devas* or gods. The Incarnations of God that we know of came later. Idol worship is also entirely absent. There were no temples in those days. All that came later. However, there are occasional references to Brahma, Vishnu and Siva or Rudra even though, as mentioned earlier, there were no idols or temples dedicated to them. In the Upanishads, there is no concept of eternal heaven or hell. The Upanishads begin with profound questions about us as human beings and about the end of all knowledge.

Some of these questions include the following: Commanded and directed by whom does the mind go towards its objects? Commanded by whom does the life-force, the first (cause), move? At whose will do men utter speech? What power directs the eye and the ear?[2] There are questions about where we came from, how life is manifested in us and so on. The Prasna Upanishad literally means the 'Question Upanishad' and has six questions. The Mundaka Upanishad begins with a question about the end of knowledge: 'What is that by knowing which all this becomes known?' This is a penetrating question. By virtue of prior understanding, the student has concluded that knowing one thing after another is an endless endeavour. He has faith or some intuition that such knowledge is possible. However, he does not know what that is and asks the teacher to explain it.

There is no reference to any religion, prophet, God or system of philosophy. The questions are always put by the earnest student to the teacher or *guru*. The word 'Upanishad' is derived from this idea—a student 'sitting down near' the teacher. When the Upanishads were composed, there were no large universities and such learning was imparted to the few earnest students who came seeking knowledge. The students lived with the *guru* for several years.

The Upanishads are in the Jnana Kanda of the Vedas. The word '*jnana*' or 'knowledge' does not mean knowledge derived from books, intellectual knowledge or even a firm grasp of essential concepts about something. It refers to knowledge gained in revelation about who we are as human beings and our relation to the Universe and that which is beyond our mind and senses—*avang manasa gochara*. However such knowledge can only be perceived by the pure mind. This Ultimate Knowledge is not far away, it is everywhere, it permeates everything. The Isa Upanishad begins with the verse '*Isa vasyam idam sarvam*', meaning that the Cosmic Principle resides in everything.

This knowledge transforms us and brings great peace, bliss or joy. This is permanent and not fleeting like our ordinary life experiences. This knowledge also delivers us from the repeated cycle of birth and death and gives *moksha* (salvation) and *mukti* (freedom). The interesting point to be noted is that this is achieved here and now, in this life and not after death. The Purusha Suktam says '*Amritam iha bhavati*', which means 'immortality is here'. The Brihadaranyaka and the Katha Upanishads say:

यदा सर्वे प्रमुच्यन्ते कामा येऽस्य हृदि श्रिताः |
अथ मर्त्योऽमृतो भवत्यत्र ब्रह्म समश्नुते ||

yadā sarve pramucyante kāmā ye'sya hṛdi śritāḥ |
atha martyo'mṛto bhavatyatra brahma samaśnute ||

[When every desire in the heart of a man hath been loosened from its moorings, then this mortal becomes immortal; even here he enjoys Brahman in this human body.]

Another central idea is that Man is divine in the sense that the Ultimate Reality is within us. Some other religions also refer to this idea: for instance, Christ's statement that the 'Kingdom of God is within you' or the well-known saying of the Persian sage Sufi Mansur Al-Hallaj, who said, '*Anal haq*', meaning 'I am the Truth'.

Human beings are also given a very exalted position. The Svetasvatara Upanishad says, '*Shrinwantu vishwe amritasya putrah*' or Listen, Oh Children of Immortality, the world over.

In summary, the Upanishads are 'revealed texts' or scriptures and form the central core of the spiritual content of Hinduism. Sometimes, the Upanishads are also known as Atmavidya (knowledge of the Self) or Brahmavidya (knowledge of Brahman).

Preliminary Details

Unlike the voluminous Samhita and Brahmanas, the Upanishads are comparatively short. The Mandukya Upanishad has only twelve *shlokas* or verses while the Isa Upanishad has eighteen verses. The longest Upanishads are the Brihadaranyaka and the Chandogya. In the Muktika Upanishad of the Shukla Yajur Veda, there is a reference to 108 Upanishads. Other references put the number at 250, although only 108 texts are extant today. Ten of them are called the Principal Upanishads. Put together, they have less than 1500 verses. By contrast, the Rig Veda Samhita alone has over 10,000 verses. The other *shlokas* or verses in the Brahmanas and Aranyakas in the Vedas are far more in number.

Though short in length, the Upanishads have many commentaries written on them. The shortest of them—the Mandukya, consisting of twelve verses—has a Mandukya *Karika* or 'explanation' of 215 verses, which was written many centuries later by Gaudapada, reputed to be the *guru* of Adi Sankara's *guru*. Later, Adi Sankara wrote a commentary ('*bhashya*') on both the Mandukya Upanishad as well as the Karika. Subsequently, Anandagiri wrote a lengthy *tika*, explaining Sankara's *bhashya*. Similarly, all the Principal Upanishads have commentaries by many *acharyas* and scholars. In contrast, there are no lengthy commentaries on the Karma Kanda. The Upanishads are highly condensed verses or *mantras* and require long explanations by later scholars. But in another sense, they are highly intuitive where the essence of the *mantra* is grasped by intuition. We shall see examples of this later.

There is a loose classification of the 108 Upanishads into the Principal Upanishads, Samanya (general), Saiva, Vaishnava, Sakta (Divine Mother), Yoga and Sannyasa Upanishads. The authorship of most of the Upanishads is not known. In this discussion, we will draw primarily upon the Principal Upanishads. They are the most universal. The Saiva, Vaishnava and Sakta Upanishads teach the Truth through a particular deity.

Scholars differ on the dates when the Upanishads were composed. It is more likely that they were part of an oral tradition and were written down later. Later, other texts also emerged which are known as Upanishads but which may have been composed after the Vedic period. By common consent among the orthodox, the earlier texts listed in the Muktika Upanishad are regarded as part of the Vedas and are in the Jnana Kanda.

Some Essential Concepts

Some important terms and concepts require clarification before we can understand the essence of the Upanishads. Such 'understanding' is mental or intellectual rather than the direct perception or revelation that the Upanishads speak of.

One important term used repeatedly is 'Brahman'. The use of the term 'Brahman' here has nothing to do with caste or any individual as used in day-to-day interactions. The root word '*brih*' means vast, expansive, all-pervasive. Brahman is the Ultimate Reality. There are two well-known definitions regarding its meaning. One is that Brahman is *Sat-Chit-Ananda*.[3] This means that Brahman is of the very essence or nature of '*Sat*' (Existence), '*Chit*' (Knowledge) and '*Ananda*' (Bliss). Thus, Brahman is Existence–Knowledge–Bliss. An alternative translation suggests that Brahman is the One Being of the very nature of Consciousness and Love, where 'Being' implies Existence, 'Consciousness' gives Knowledge, and 'Love' gives Bliss. This Existence–Consciousness–Bliss is the effect of the Being whose very nature is Love and Consciousness. Another well-known definition is *Satyam-Jnanam-Anantam* Brahma.[4] Brahman is Truth ('*Satyam*'), Knowledge ('*Jnanam*') and

Infinity ('*Anantam*'). There are several commentaries on this phrase as well. 'Truth' is that which always is, never changes and is eternal. It of course includes telling the truth. Knowledge here as in the earlier definition, means the very source or essence of all knowledge—by knowing which all else is known. *Anantam* or 'Infinity' goes beyond the usually understood meaning of infinite space and time. It is also beyond any mental conception limited by space and time.

Other descriptions of Brahman include 'unborn', 'un-decaying', 'undying' and 'immortal'. Brahman is beyond anything that the mind can imagine. It is eternal, unchanging, imperishable, self-luminous, beyond time and space, infinite. It is the source from which the world originated, that in which the world exists and into which the world dissolves.

It is said that Brahman cannot be defined as it has no attributes. However, it can be argued that Existence, Truth, Infinitude, Consciousness and Bliss are not attributes but the very nature of Brahman. There are others who have said that Brahman does indeed have attributes. These include, for instance, omniscience and omnipotence. At the same time, it is often reiterated in the Upanishads that Brahman cannot be described. It can only be experienced or, even beyond that, one can become one with It. However, the two definitions are given and help us to understand what the Upanishads are saying.

Another term is 'Atman', usually referred to as the 'Self' in English. The Atman is not the ego or our thoughts. It is of the very nature of Brahman, is present in every living being and is realized or eventually known by the individual. Another term is 'Purusha'. The word 'Purusha' occurs several times in the Vedic Samhitas as well as later in the Bhagavad Gita. It is also used in the Sankhya philosophy in contrast to 'Prakriti' where 'Purusha' refers to the Soul and 'Prakriti' refers to nature. Purusha is used over the centuries with slightly different meanings in different texts. In the Upanishadic sense, it means the Atman. There are other terms such as '*nirguna*' (without qualities) Brahman and '*saguna*' (with qualities) Brahman, and there are different terms for different grades of realization. However, these classifications came much later and will be discussed when we discuss the philosophies. Often, the word '*Tat*'—translated as 'That'—is used to indicate the Supreme Brahman.

A human being has a soul* and is called a '*jiva*'. Human beings reap the consequences of their actions. This is also called '*karma*'. As mentioned earlier, '*karma*' has at least three connotations. One is the Vedic *karmas* which include the

---

* In fact, all living beings, whether animal or plant, have a soul. One famous verse goes even further and says that '*Sarvam khalvidam Brahma*', meaning 'everything is Brahman'. This includes inanimate objects and perhaps also implies thoughts, dreams, ideas and concepts. In other words, there is nothing except Brahman.

rituals such as *sandhyavandana* (the prayers in the morning and evening), *homa* (Vedic sacrifice) and so on. Although these *karmas* confer benefits, including purification of the being, they do not lead directly to Ultimate Knowledge. Another meaning of *karma* is 'action' and includes the consequences of those actions. These consequences create impressions on the mind and become the cause of further action. For instance, an action that leads to pleasant consequences creates a favourable impression in the mind. At some later point, this impression causes us to repeat that action. A third meaning of *karma* is the total set of actions done by a person whose impressions are in the mind and eventually cause him to either act upon them or face the consequences. It is generally implied that good actions lead to good or pleasant impressions and bad actions to bad or unpleasant impressions.

'*Moksha*' means 'liberation'. It implies liberation from birth and death, from desire, from the senses, from attachment and gives bliss and joy. '*Mukti*' is a very similar term and means 'freedom'. Such freedom also implies freedom from the cycle of birth and death as well as from desires and attachments. Other terms which are used include '*kaivalya*' (literally, 'being alone with one's own Self or Brahman'), meaning 'liberation'; '*amrutam*' (literally, 'that which does not die'), meaning 'immortality'. As mentioned earlier, the phrase '*amrutam iha bhavati*' means that liberation or immortality is here and now. Thus, there are many words which are used to convey a very similar meaning.

All the Upanishads begin with invocatory short prayers for peace which are called the *shanti mantras*. Such *mantras* are also there in the Karma Kanda of the Vedas. They prepare the mind for studying the Upanishads. Some of the well-known *shanti mantras* are given below and are taken from the ten Principal Upanishads.

Three of the Principal Upanishads—the Taittiriya, Katha and Svetaswatara—have another invocatory prayer that does not invoke any of the Vedic gods. This is the prayer of the student and the teacher:

ॐ सह नाववतु |
सह नौ भुनक्तु |
सह वीर्यं करवावहै |
तेजस्विनावधीतमस्तु मा विद्विषावहै ||
ॐ शान्तिः शान्तिः शान्तिः ||

Om sahanavavatu
saha nau bhunaktu
Sahaviryam karavavahai
Tejasvinavadhi tamastu maa vidvishavahai
Om Shanti, Shanti Shanti

A free translation is as follows: 'Om! May we both be protected; may we be nourished; may we work together with energy; may our study be vigorous and effective; may we not mutually dislike each other. Om, Peace, Peace, Peace.'

A famous invocatory prayer in the Isa and Brihadaranyaka Upanishads runs as follows:

ॐ पूर्णमदः पूर्णमिदम् पूर्णात् पूर्णमुदच्यते |
पूर्णस्य पूर्णमादाय पूर्णमेवावशिष्यते ||
ॐ शान्तिः शान्तिः शान्तिः ||

Om pūrṇam adaḥ pūrṇam idam pūrṇāt pūrṇam udacyate
pūrṇasya pūrṇam ādāya pūrṇam evāvaśiṣyate
Om śāntiḥ śāntiḥ śāntiḥ

The word '*purna*' means 'whole' and denotes the entire Universe, including everything in it and beyond it. The word 'infinity' is usually used for *purna*. A free translation is: 'That is Infinite, this is Infinite, Infinity comes (or emanates) from Infinity. If you take Infinity from Infinity, then Infinity alone remains. Om Peace, Peace, Peace.'

This *mantra* is chanted more often since it does not invoke any deities or gods.

Suggested Method of Studying the Upanishads

Unlike the lengthy Vedic Samhitas and Brahmanas, it is possible even today to read the Upanishads with some knowledge of the meaning of the Sanskrit words. Several translations are easily available. Perhaps one way of studying the Upanishads is to recall that they are Universal, Eternal and Impersonal. For instance, one of the great sayings or *'mahavakyas'* in the Upanishads (the Aitareya Upanishad of the Rig Veda) is *'Prajnanam Brahma'*, which simply means that Consciousness is Brahman. Lengthy commentaries have been written on this one terse saying. However, this is an example of something that is universal, eternal and impersonal. In contrast, a particular ritual or mode of worship may be useful but may not be universally applicable. Wherever there are such non-universal references in the Upanishads or any scripture, we need to take them as symbolic illustrations that were appropriate for those time. For example, the sun is often used as a symbol for illumination. The well-known *shloka 'Vedahametam Purusha mantam adityavarnam'*, means 'I have known that Supreme Purusha (or Atman), brilliant like the Sun'. Here Sun does not refer to the physical Sun in the sky. The symbols need to be interpreted correctly to understand their spiritual significance. Fortunately, most of the translations do that. If we recall the universal, impersonal and eternal aspects of the Upanishads, it may be easier to grasp the essential meaning of the texts.

Principal Contents of the Upanishads

One central idea in the Upanishads is that the Atman is present in every human being or, rather, in all living creatures. Several well-known Upanishadic aphorisms or verses proclaim this. The well-known *mahavakyas* or 'great sayings' say that each individual has the same spark of divinity. *Aham Bramhasmi* ('I am Brahman'), *Tattvam Asi* ('Thou art That') and *Ayam Atma Brahma* ('This Soul or Self is Brahman'). The Svetasvatara Upanishad addresses the whole world by saying, '*Shrinwantu vishwe amritasya putrah*' or 'Listen, Oh Children of Immortality, the world over.'

Closely related to this idea is that everyone can know this Atman or Brahman. An essential Upanishadic idea is 'look not for the truth in any religion; it is here in the human soul'.[5] The Kaivalya Upanishad says '*Tattvam eva, Tvameva Tat*', meaning That alone Thou art, Thou Art That Alone' giving it emphasis by repetition. The Isa Upanishad says, 'Thou Sun, who hast covered the Truth with thy golden disc, do thou remove the veil, so that I may see the Truth that is within thee. I have known the Truth that is within thee, I have known what the real meaning of thy rays and thy glory is and have seen That which shines in thee; the Truth in thee I see, and That which is within thee is within me, and I am That.'[6] A famous aphorism or *sutra* is the *mahavakya* '*Tat-tvam-asi*' or 'Thou art That' from the Chandogya Upanishad. The teacher, Uddalaka Aruni tells his student Svetaketu—who is also his son—that he is, in essence, the Supreme Brahman, not just once but at least nine times. The lessons taught by Uddalaka will help Svetaketu to eventually know that for himself.

The Upanishads also emphasize the Oneness of life and the Oneness of everything. The phrase '*Sarvam Khalvidam Brahma*' from the Chandogya Upanishad literally means 'All this is Brahman', implying that the whole Universe is pervaded by Brahman. The phrase '*Isa vasyam Idam Sarvam*' from the Isa Upanishad means that the Divine Isa or Ishwara dwells in all this. If the Atman is in everyone and Brahman pervades everything, then we must all be One. Later commentators have said that the basis of all ethics comes from this concept of oneness. Since we are all one, we should serve each other, help each other, not hurt each other and so on, because others are not separate from me.

Some philosophers say that Atman and Brahman are not identical. They say that Brahman is qualified by the world and the living being. Others say that Brahman is separate from the world and from living beings. However, all agree that Brahman exists, and that it is of the nature of Existence–Knowledge–Bliss and that living beings are either identical to it, part of it or reflections of it.

Selected Verses from the Upanishads

Some of the most quoted verses, *shlokas* or *mantras* from the Upanishads help us to get a feel for what they contain. Some of the poetic verses are given below. They are often quoted because they are considered to be revelations. They are not regarded as metaphysical speculations about the Universe but as direct revelations or realizations of sages in higher states of consciousness. Such a realization is possible for any earnest aspirant.

न तत्र सुर्यो भाति न चंन्द्रतारकं नेमा विद्युतो भान्ति कुतोऽयमग्निः |
तमेव भान्तमनुभाति सर्वं तस्य भासा सर्वमिदं विभाति ||

Na tatra Suryo bhati, na chandratarakam, nema vidyuto bhanti, kutoyamagnih,
Tameva Bhantam anubhati sarvam, tasya bhasa sarvam idam vibhati

[There the sun doth not shine, neither the moon, nor stars, nor lightning, what to speak of this fire. That shining, everything doth shine. Through That everything shineth.]

—Katha Upanishad, translation by Swami Vivekananda. This identical verse is also in the Mundaka Upanishad

अथ यदतः परो दिवो ज्योतिर्दीप्यते विश्वतः पृष्ठेषु सर्वतः पृष्ठेष्वनुत्तमेषूत्तमेषु लोकेष्विदं वाव तद्यदिदमस्मिन्नन्तः पुरुषो ज्योतिस्तस्यैषा

Atha yadatah paro divo jyotir deepyate vishvataha prishtheshu sarvatah

43

Prishthevan uttameshuttameshu lokeshvidam vaava taddadidamasmin anantah purusho jyotistasyaisha

[Now that light which shines above this heaven, higher than all, higher than everything, in the highest world, beyond which there are no other worlds, that is the same light which is within man.]

—Chandogya Upanishad 3.13.7,
translated by Max Mueller

यावान्वा अयमाकाशस्तावानेषोऽन्तर्हृदय अकाश उभे अस्मिन्द्यावापृथिवी अन्तरेव समाहिते उभावग्निश्च वायुश्च सूर्याचन्द्रमसावुभौ विद्युन्नक्षत्राणि यच्चास्येहास्ति यच्च नास्ति सर्वं तदस्मिन्समाहितमिति || ८.१.३ ||

Yāvānvā ayamākāśastāvāneṣo'ntarhṛdaya akāśa ubhe asmindyāvāpṛthivī antareva samāhite ubhāvagniśca vāyuśca sūryācandramasāvubhau vidyunnakṣatrāṇi yaccāsyehāsti yacca nāsti sarvaṃ tadasminsamāhitamiti || 8.1.3 ||

[The little space within the heart is as great as the vast Universe. The heavens and the earth are there, and the sun and the moon and the stars. Fire and lightning and winds are there, and all that now is and all that is not.]

—Chandogya Upanishad,
translation by Swami Prabhavananda

यो वै भूमा तत्सुखं नाल्पे सुखमस्ति भूमैव सुखं . . .

Yo vai bhūmā tatsukhaṃ nālpe sukhamasti bhūmaiva sukham

[That which is infinite is the source of happiness. There is no happiness in the finite. Happiness is only in the infinite.]

—Chandogya Upanishad

असतो मा सद्गमय । तमसो मा ज्योतिर्गमय ।
मृत्योर्मा अमृतं गमय । ॐ शान्तिः शान्तिः शान्तिः ॥

Asatō mā sadgamaya, tamasō mā jyōtirgamaya
mṛtyōrmā amṛtaṃ gamaya, Om śāntiḥ śāntiḥ śāntiḥ

[From untruth lead us to Truth, from darkness lead us to Light.
From death lead us to Immortality. Om Peace, Peace, Peace.]

—Brihadaranyaka Upanishad 1.3.28

काममय एवायं पुरुष इति । सा यथाकामो भवति तत्क्रतुर भवति ॥
यात्क्रतुर भवति तत कर्म कुरुते । यत कर्म कुरुते तद् अभिसम पद्यते ॥

Kamamaya Evaya Purusha Iti; Sa Yathakamo Bhavati
Tatkraturbhavati

Yatkratur bhavati Tat karma krurute; yat karma kurute tad abhisam padyate.

[You are what your deep, driving desire is; As your desire is, so is your will.
As your will is, so is your deed; As your deed is, so is your destiny.]

—Brihadaraṇyaka Upanishad 4.4.5

न जायते म्रियते वा विपश्चिन्नायं कुतश्चिन्न बभूव कश्चित् ।
अजो नित्यः शाश्वतोऽयं पुराणो न हन्यते हन्यमाने शरीरे ॥

Na jāyate mriyate vā vipaścin nāyaṁ kutaścin na babhūvā kaścit | ajo nityaḥ śāśvato'yam purāṇo na hanyate hanyamāne śarīre ||

[The Self is never born; nor does it die. It did not originate from anything and nothing originates from it. It is unborn, eternal, abiding and primeval. It is not slain when the body is slain.*]

—Katha Upanishad 18

आनन्दो ब्रह्मेति व्यजानात् । आनन्दाध्येव खल्विमानि
भूतानि जायन्ते । आनन्देन जातानि जीवन्ति ।
आनन्दं प्रयन्त्यभिसंविशन्तीति ।

---

* An almost identical verse can be found in the Bhagavad Gita which came later.

Ānando brahmeti vyajānāt . ānandādhyeva khalvimāni
bhūtāni jāyante | ānandena jātāni jīvanti |
ānandaṃ prayantyabhisaṃviśantīti ||

[Bliss is Brahman; from bliss beings are born;
by bliss, when born, they live; into bliss they enter at
their death.]

—Taittiriya Upanishad 3.6

Some Recurring Themes in the Upanishads

Some of the important themes that recur in all the Upanishads are presented in this section. This helps to grasp the essence of what they say. These themes include sound syllables, especially the sacred *mantra* 'Om', the theme of light as a symbol of enlightenment, the Atman residing in the heart of the human aspirant and the repeated references to joy or bliss. They also refer to meditation as a means for realizing the highest Truth. It is worth noting that all these themes of sound, light, the heart, joy, meditation and truth are also practical means suggested by the Upanishads to be used by the aspirant. For instance, meditating on the blissful light in the heart while repeating the syllable Om is one such method. While affirming that the individual Atman and Brahman are one and the same, the Upanishads also emphasize that Brahman is vast, all-pervading.

Sound

All the Principal Upanishads refer repeatedly to the word symbol 'Om'. Some say that Om is Brahman. The Mandukya Upanishad says, *'Om-ityedat aksharam idam sarvam'*, or 'Om is the Imperishable and is all this'. The Taittirya Upanishad says Om is Brahman, Om is all this. In the same verse it goes on to repeat Om nine times. The Katha Upanishad says this Imperishable Om is Brahman. The Prasna Upanishad says, 'This, O Satyakama, is the lower and higher Brahman and is Om.' The Mundaka Upanishad says, 'Meditate on the Atman or Self with the help of Om.' The Maitri Upanishad says, 'Meditate on the Self as Om.' The Chandogya Upanishad says, 'Om indeed is all these.'[7]

The human mind is sensitive to sound. The Upanishads discovered that meditating on a sound symbol that includes the whole Universe is a powerful aid to meditation. The idea of sacred syllables is also there in other religions. Om is used in Buddhism as well with the well-known *mantra* *'Om mani padme hum'*, which means 'Om, the jewel in the Heart, (*'hum'* is another sacred syllable). The Christians use 'Amen' which sounds similar to Om. Islam and Judaism also have a tradition of repeating the sacred syllable *'Amin'*.

---

* The Bhagavad Gita, which came later, says *'Om iti Brahma'*, which can be translated as 'Om is Brahman'.

Light

Another theme is that of light. Some verses refer to the
light in the heart of every being and ask the aspirant to
meditate on it. The Isa Upanishad says, 'In the Golden
Vessel is the face of Truth.' It also refers to the rays of
light which are bright. The Mundaka Upanishad uses the
phrases 'beyond the golden sheath' and *'jyotisham jyoti'*,
meaning 'the light of lights'. Following a series of verses
about this idea of light, it proceeds to the famous verse
quoted earlier which says 'There the sun does not shine,
nor the moon, nor lightning, nor this fire. By that Light,
everything is illuminated'. It also says that Brahman is in
the heart, self-effulgent and beyond thought. The Prasna
Upanishad uses the phrases 'the thousand rays' and 'the
one Light'. The Taittirya Upanishad says 'that Immortality
is effulgent.' One of the most frequently quoted verses on
this idea is from the Chandogya Upanishad. It says, 'That
light which shines above this heaven, higher than all, higher
than everything, in the highest world, beyond which there
are no other worlds, that is the same light which is within
man' (translation by Max Mueller).[*][8]

The human mind is sensitive not only to sound but
to sight as well. Light as a symbol is universal and non-
sectarian. The revelations in the Upanishads point to this

[*] The Bhagavad Gita uses the term *jyotishām api taj jyoti*—the Light of
all Lights.

light that is perceived in revelation and hint that it can also act as an aid to meditation for the seeker. The Gayatri Mantra is also a meditation on light. In popular language, when we say that someone is illumined. This also refer to light.

Atman in the Heart

The Upanishads also clearly say that the Atman is within the heart of all beings. The Mundaka Upanishad says, '*Antah sarire jyotirmayo hi subhro*', '[It is] in the body, that Light that is pure'. The Prasna Upanishad says this Atman resides in the heart. It also says 'here in this body, O Soumya, is this Purusha'. '*Soumya*' is often used by the teacher addressing the student and means 'worthy one, amiable, good looking'. The Taittirya Upanishad says 'That (Atman) is in the heart space. That Purusha can be realized through knowledge.' The Katha Upanishad says the Atman resides in the Heart of all beings. It also says the Atman 'of the size of a thumb, in the body resides that Atman, in the Heart.' This also indicates a method of meditation on the Atman in the heart.[9]

Joy and Bliss

Perhaps one of the most appealing aspects of the Upanishads is that of joy or bliss. The Taittirya Upanishad in particular has a whole section called Brahmanandavalli or the Bliss of Brahman. One phrase is '*raso vai sah*', which means That (Brahman) is full of *rasa*. '*Rasa*' is a word which is difficult to translate into English since it is used in many different contexts. In this case, however, it refers to Brahman as full of joy. In a series of verses, it tries to convey that Bliss of Brahman. The Brihadaranyaka Upanishad has almost identical verses. It begins with a young man full of health and vigour and with the wealth of the whole world. That is one unit of Bliss. A hundred times that is the Bliss of the divine Gandharvas; a hundred times that is for the manes (souls of departed ancestors); a hundred times of that for the gods in heaven; a hundred times that for the *Karma Devas*; a hundred times that for the gods; a hundred times that for Indra (the king of the gods); a hundred times for Brihaspati, the teacher or *guru* of Indra; a hundred times that for Virat, who has the Three Worlds for his body; and a hundred times that for *Hiranmayagarbha* or the manifest Brahman. Although the allusions to various deities are difficult to comprehend today, the central message of the verses is clear. The Bliss of Brahman is several orders of magnitude beyond anything we can experience or even imagine. Other phrases used elsewhere in the same Upanishad are 'that blissful Self' and 'he who knows the Bliss of Brahman'. It goes on to say that we are born from Bliss, live in Bliss and return to Bliss in the end.

The Brihadaranyaka Upanishad says 'This is that Supreme Bliss. On a particle of this Bliss the beings live.' It uses the phrase 'Brahman is Knowledge and Bliss'. The Mundaka Upanishad says 'That Self (Atman or Brahman) shines as Bliss.'[10]

Meditation

There are references to meditation as well. The Mundaka Upanishad says 'seek the Indivisible through meditation' and also 'This subtle Self is to be known through the pure mind or Consciousness.' It goes on to say 'meditate on the Atman or Self through Om alone'. The Katha Upanishad says, 'This Om is imperishable when known [through meditation and] gives That (Brahman) to the aspirant.'[11]

Truth

Truth or Satya is used repeatedly in the Upanishads. The word 'satya' comes from the root 'Sat', meaning 'that which "Is"', usually translated as 'existence'. The Mundaka Upanishad says 'Satyena labhya', meaning 'through Truth is attained [the Atman or Self]'. It has the phrase Satyameva jayate', meaning 'Truth alone triumphs.' It adds that the satyena pantha or the Path of Truth leads to 'satyasya paramaṃ nidhānam', that is the Supreme Treasure (Brahman) which is the result of following the Truth. The word '*satya*' occurs three times in the same verse giving emphasis to truth. The Brihadaranyaka Upanishad says that *dharma* and truth are the same. It uses the phrase '*Satyasya satya*', meaning 'the Truth of Truths'. One of the definitions of Brahman in the Taittiriya Upanishad is '*Satyam, Jnanam, Anantam*' or Truth, Knowledge and Infinity. It also has the injunction or prayer '*Satyam vada, dharmam chara*', which can be translated as 'Speak the Truth, follow the *dharma* (right conduct)'.

All-Pervading

There are several references to Brahman being all-pervading. The Isa Upanishad says '*Isa vasyam idam sarvam*' which means that Isa or Ishwara (the manifestation of Brahman) pervades everything. The Mandukya Upanishad says that '*Sarvaṃ hyetad brahma, ayam atma Brahma*', or 'All this is that Brahman'. This is followed by the well-known *mahavakya* that Atman is Brahman. The Prasna Upanishad says '*viswarupam harinam*', i.e., of the form of the Universe, full of rays. The Mundaka says 'Purusha *evedam visvam*', the Purusha alone is all this.

Conclusions

The key recurring themes in all the Upanishads are:

1. There is a Supreme Reality known as Brahman which is eternal, changeless, all-knowing, all-pervasive. Two common ways of describing It are *Sat-Chit-Ananda* Brahman, that is, Brahman is Existence-Knowledge-Bliss, and *Satyam–Jnanam–Anantam* Brahman, that is, Brahman is Truth–Knowledge–Infinity.

2. This Brahman can be realized here and now by earnest aspirants. Such a realization makes us blissful and takes us beyond all sorrow. It also frees us from the cycle of birth and death.

3. The individual soul—known as Atman—is present in every living and being can be realized.

4. This Atman is the same as Brahman. The idea being that there is the One Infinite, and there cannot be two.

The teachings of the Upanishads are not denominational and does not require prior belief or faith. An interest in knowing the truth and a willingness to implement the ideas are all that is required. This has perhaps attracted the attention of a large number of people around the world.*

Since different sages have, at different points of time, presented the same ideas in different Upanishads,

---

* Examples include Max Mueller, Paul Duessen, Arthur Avalon, John Woodruffe, Arthur Schopenhauer, Herman Hesse, J. Robert Oppenheimer, Erwin Schrödinger, Christopher Isherwood and Romain Rolland from outside India and Adi Sankara, Swami Vivekananda, Sivananda, Aurobindo and many others from India.

these revelations are not unique. The key idea perhaps is that knowing or realizing something that is beyond our daily experience can free us from sorrow, give bliss and knowledge.

Later commentators have given metaphysical theories to explain these simple ideas. However, they have also said that for he who knows all this in the real sense, all arguments and disputations cease. There is no need for metaphysics or philosophy.

Only a preliminary glimpse into the Upanishads is given here. They give a brief idea about why these scriptures occupy the highest position in Hinduism. The Upanishads are a living tradition and the texts are studied by ardent seekers even today. Many commentaries have been written on these scriptures in Sanskrit, English and various other languages. Here, the attempt has been to try and offer an insight into what the scriptures say. Only the main ideas have been introduced here. However, later commentaries written by many reputed scholars and sages throw much greater light on these scriptures. Those interested in further study should consult these texts. It is usually said that these texts should be studied in depth from a learned teacher.

Some Notes

The Upanishads have been translated into several languages including English, Spanish, Latin, French, German, Italian,

Dutch, Polish, Japanese, Russian, Urdu and Persian. Apart from the philosophical content, they are non-sectarian and are largely universal and impersonal. This makes it appealing the world over in contrast to later Hindu customs and rituals which are based on specific cultural practices and various temples, gods, worship and so on. Historians such as Will Durant have observed, 'The Upanishads are as old as Homer and as modern as Kant.'[12] Max Mueller, Paul Duessen, Arthur Schopenhauer, Ralph Waldo Emerson, Romain Rolland, Aldous Huxley, Christopher Isherwood, Emperor Akbar, his grandson Dara Shikoh and several others had high regard for the Upanishads. Some modern scientists and physicists such as J. Robert Oppenheimer and Erwin Schrödinger were also deeply influenced by the Upanishads.

The phrase सत्यमेव जयते (*Satyameva jayate*) means 'Truth alone triumphs.' It is from the Mundaka Upanishad, one of the ten Principal Upanishads. It is written in the Sanskrit or Devanagari script and can be found on the plinth of the emblem of India. It consists of four lions looking in four directions and was created by Emperor Asoka thousands of years ago. The same phrase is thereon all the currency notes and coins used in present-day India.

3

IMPORTANT CONCEPTS IN HINDUISM

As we move ahead from the Vedic period, we see that the scriptures begin to discuss metaphysical and philosophical concepts. To understand them we need to have a clear understanding of these concepts. Broadly, there are two types of these later scriptures. One has philosophy or metaphysics. Among the philosophical texts, there are the Brahma Sutras, the Bhagavad Gita and even later texts on the Advaita, Visishtadvaita and Dvaita philosophies. The other scriptural texts are about worship, practice, ritual and mythology.

One difficulty arises in attempting to precisely define these concepts. They are used over the centuries in different texts in different contexts and have acquired slightly different meanings. However, we will attempt to define these terms based on the most widely accepted meaning today.

The first important concept is that of God. In the Upanishads, the reference is to Brahman, defined as *Sat-Chit-Ananda Brahma* (Brahman as Existence–Knowledge–Bliss) or as *Satyam–Jnanam–Anantam Brahma* (Brahman as Truth–Knowledge–Infinity). These descriptions are about the *nirakara* (formless) and *nirguna* (without attributes) Brahman which does not have any qualities. The idea is that anything that has a form or attribute is limited. Such an abstract concept is perhaps difficult to grasp, but this is precisely what the *rishis* realized and described. The term '*Alakh Niranjan*' is used in the Guru Granth Sahib, the holy book of the Sikhs, and denotes the same concept. Buddhism also says that *Nirvana*—the state of salvation and of egolessness cannot be described.

Brahman is also understood by later philosophies as *saguna,* with attributes. These include controller or Lord of the Universe, Omniscience and Omnipotence.

Next, we have the concept of God as Ishwara.* Literally, '*Ish*' means lord, master or ruler and '*vara*' means the best or supreme. Ishwara is generally considered to be the Creator of the universe and also the *phaladata*, that is, the giver of the fruits of action. The essential laws that govern the workings of the universe and the chain of cause

---

* If the universe is understood to mean all phenomenal existence— physical, temporal, spatial, mental, emotional, dream and whatever other worlds that may exist even beyond space and time—then we can use the term 'universe' instead of 'phenomenal existence'.

and effect originate from Ishwara.* Ishwara is formless but has the twin roles of creation and governance of all phenomenal existence. Ishwara emanates from Brahman and is not separate from it. In other texts, the word *shakti* or Divine Mother is used as the One who creates and governs the universe. When inactive, Brahman is thought of as *nirguna* or without attributes, and when it is active in creating and governing the universe, it is thought of as *saguna,* with attributes. According to one view, *saguna* Brahman is Ishwara. Brahman is thus the selfsame Reality that has both aspects—the inactive and the active. Ishwara is also formless, or alternately can take innumerable forms. The Vaishnava traditions use the term 'Bhagavan' for God. Other terms that are equivalent to God are *Parameshwara* (the Supreme Ishwara) and *Paramatma* (the Supreme Atman).

Brahman can be inactive and passive as the formless, attribute-less Absolute Reality and also be the creator, sustainer and law-giver of the universe. The paradox that Brahman can be formless and also have innumerable forms is also unique to Hinduism. Since Brahman is One, the same reality can be inactive and active, formless and with

---

* The idea of God or Ishwara in the ancient texts is accepted whole heartedly only by two of the six major philosophies or darsanas. These will be discussed in more detail in a subsequent chapter on Philosophies or Darsanas.

all forms of the universe. Later philosophies or *darsanas* have debated and discussed the concept of Ishwara and there are differences amongst them. We will discuss these in a later chapter.

A more philosophical concept of Ishwara-as-Creator is there in the Vedas and Upanishads. The Aitareya Upanishad proclaims, 'Om! In the beginning, the Atman alone existed. There was nothing else whatsoever. It thought "Let me create the worlds".' The Mundaka Upanishad says '*Om! Brahma devanam prathamah sambhuva, vishwasya karta bhuvanasya gopta*', which means 'Om! Brahma the first Manifestation, Creator and Protector of the universe.' The Mundaka Upanishad says that the Atman or Self is the origin of all the manifest world and phenomenal existence. Thus, the underlying idea here is that Ishwara emanates from Brahman.

The different schools of philosophy have different views about God. The Sankhya, Vaiseshika and Purva Mimamsa are either silent about God, regard the concept as irrelevant or reject it entirely. Nyaya has debated this concept, with later scholars accepting the idea of God. The Yoga and Uttara Mimamsa philosophies have explicitly accepted the idea of God. Thus, the six *darsanas* or philosophies differ among themselves on God. The later

---

* In Hinduism, *darsanas* are philosophies. Six of them survive and are discussed in a later chapter.

philosophies such as the Advaita, Visishtadvaita and Dvaita also differ on the concept of Ishwara. This is discussed in detail in a subsequent chapter on 'Philosophy'. Yet other philosophies (such as the Charvaka) are materialistic and reject the notion of God.

One can see that it is difficult to precisely define what God is according to the scriptures. However, in popular practice, large numbers of people do believe in God. God has three aspects: Brahma (not to be confused with the Absolute Brahman of the Upanishads) as the Creator of the universe, Vishnu as the Sustainer and Protector of the universe and Rudra or Siva as the Dissolver of the universe. In the Shaivaite tradition, Siva is viewed as the God of the *yogis* who destroys the evil within us, purifies us and leads us to Brahman. Taken together, Brahma, Vishnu and Siva are known as the *Trimurtis* or the Three Gods. They have various stories, legends and mythologies surrounding them which are outlined in detail in the scriptures called the Puranas. In addition, there are many other gods and goddesses. The consorts of these three—Saraswati (Goddess of Learning), Lakshmi (Goddess of Wealth) and Parvati (the Divine Mother manifesting *shakti* or power and energy)—are also worshipped as divine. There are literally millions of other deities. These gods and goddesses, although apparently never born on earth, have a human aspect, form and qualities. They can be worshipped and there are temples dedicated to them. There are other gods and goddesses not mentioned in any of the ancient texts for whom temples exist in different regions according to local folk beliefs and traditions. The underlying belief is that God has innumerable forms and qualities and therefore can manifest Himself or Herself in innumerable ways.

In the Vedas, there are references to various *devas* or deities such as Indra, Agni, Surya and so on. '*Deva*' literally means 'the shining one'. These *devas* are not creators of the universe and are also different from the millions of Puranic gods and goddesses. These Vedic deities are psychological forces or energies that are invoked, often through Vedic rituals, with appropriate *mantras* or sacred syllables. They can also be manifested within an individual. However, they are formless and there have never been any temples dedicated to these Vedic deities. Although these deities are not worshipped regularly today, they are nonetheless invoked whenever Vedic rituals are performed.

In the Bhagavad Gita, it is stated that it is very difficult to know the Unmanifest and that it is easier to know the Manifest or Personal God, '*kleśho dhikataras teṣhām avyaktāsakta-chetasām; avyaktā hi gatir duḥkhaṁ dehavadbhir avāpyate*'. It means that the difficulty of those who set their minds on the Unmanifest is greater as it is hard to reach for the embodied human being. It goes on to say that through this Personal God, one can reach the Unmanifest Brahman as well. The Personal God is not defined but is left to the interpretation of the aspirant.

Since such a God has a form and attributes, the devotee finds it easier to worship.

Another distinct feature of Hinduism is the idea of the *avatar* or Incarnation of God. Literally, *avatar* means descent and implies the descent of God. The formless, attribute-less Brahman takes birth and lives on earth as the *avatar*. Perhaps the only other religion that has a similar concept is Christianity, where Jesus Christ is considered to be an Incarnation of God or the Son of God. In Hinduism, however, there are many incarnations. The popular notion taken from the Garuda Purana is of ten *avatars*. Even in this list of ten *avatars*, there are variations, with some adding the Buddha as an *avatar* while others omit him. The Bhagavatam or Bhagavata Purana (distinct from the Bhagavad Gita) talks of more than twenty *avatars*. There are also references to other *avatars* elsewhere. Two of the well-known *avatars* are Rama in the historical epic Ramayana and Krishna in the Bhagavad Gita, Mahabharata and the Bhagavata Purana.

However, what is more important is the idea behind the *avatar*. The *avatar* is a fully enlightened individual who is completely identified with Brahman. They exhibit extraordinary spiritual power that other illumined sages do not. Swami Vivekananda, a modern-day saint-scholar, said, 'Avataras are Kapâlamochanas, that is, they can alter the doom of people . . . One who can alter the doom of people is the Lord. No Sadhu, however advanced, can claim this unique position.'[1] In that sense, the *avatar* plays the same role as Ishwara, the Lord of the universe—that of the *phaladata*, the one who gives the fruits of each person's actions. The *avatar* can transmit spirituality to others by a mere wish, look or touch and raise their consciousness. For instance, Krishna shows his divine form to Arjuna in the Bhagavad Gita, which overwhelms him. Another aspect is the spiritual power they bring that continues for centuries. Referring to Krishna, Vivekananda says, 'Five thousand years have passed and he has influenced millions and millions'.[2] He characterizes the Buddha as 'the most gigantic spiritual wave ever to burst upon human society'[3] and, speaking of Christ, observes, 'the three years of his ministry were like one compressed, concentrated age, which it has taken nineteen hundred years to unfold'.[4] The *avatar* is also a redeemer of humankind. Rama, another *avatar*, is often called *patita pavana*, 'the one who purifies the fallen'. Jesus is also a redeemer of the fallen. Krishna says (in the Gita, Chapter 18, verse 66), 'Surrender to Me and I will redeem you.' Over centuries and millennia, aspirants have worshipped them and followed their teachings. This does not happen in the case of other saints. Vivekananda goes on to say, 'The Omnipresent God of the universe cannot be seen until He is reflected by these giant lamps of the earth—The Prophets, the man-Gods, the Incarnations, the embodiments of God.'[5] The *avatar* is part of an ancient continuum. Referring to ancient sages,

Krishna says, 'I gave this teaching to Visvasvan, who gave it to Manu who gave it to Iksvaku.' The Buddha refers to twenty-four Buddhas before him. Referring to the ancient prophet Abraham, Christ says 'Before Abraham, I am' and also says, 'Do not think that I have come to abolish the Law or the Prophets; I have not come to abolish them but to fulfill them.'*

The terms '*jnana*', '*bhakti*', '*yoga*', '*yajna*', '*sannyasa*', '*tyaga*', '*mantra*', '*jiva*', '*japa*', '*samskara*' and '*tapas*' are used often in various scriptures. *Jnana* or knowledge has been used in the Vedas and Upanishads as well as in subsequent texts. It has different meanings or connotations, often depending upon the context. In the highest sense, it means divine knowledge or realization of God or Brahman. *Jnana* is also used to mean knowledge of any subject, whether mundane or spiritual. *Bhakti* refers to devotion to God, usually a Personal God. *Yoga* is used in a much wider variety of contexts. The root word is '*yuj*', meaning 'to yoke, join or unite'. *Yoga* thus refers to union. The word is also used in conjunction with various philosophies such as the Sankhya, Jnana, Bhakti, Raja and Karma Yogas. Physical exercises through *yoga asanas* or postures are referred to as *hathayoga*. Although it is this type of physical exercise

---

* The Prophet Mohammed, Guru Nanak and Mahavira did not refer to themselves as *avatars*, which is why they are not mentioned here. Although the Buddha also did not characterize himself as an *avatar*, some Hindu texts name him as an incarnation.

that is most often understood as *'yoga'* in the popular imagination, this is not the sense in which it is used in the scriptural texts. Related to this is the term *'yogi'*, which refers to the person who either practices one of the *yogas* or has attained the goal of unity.

Another important word is *'sannyasa'*. It refers to the renunciation of worldly pursuits by a spiritual aspirant. This tradition of renunciation is prevalent in other religions as well, such as *bhikkus** in Buddhism, *sadhus* in Jainism (and Hinduism) *sadhvis* or nuns in Jainism and monks and nuns in Christianity. *Sannyasa* is considered to have a deep meaning and there are many definitions of it. The Vedas use the term *'muni'* for the one who has given up worldly pursuits and seeks the spiritual Truth. The word *'mundaka'* in the Mundaka Upanishad means 'shaven head' and refers to those who have renounced material life. It is used often in the Bhagavad Gita. Etymologically, the root word comes from *'sam-ni-asa'*, where *'sam'* stands for 'all', *'ni'* stands for 'near' or 'below', and *'asa'* for 'throw'. It refers to complete renunciation. There is a group of Upanishads known as the Sannyasa Upanishads. The word *'sannyasi'* is used for someone who has renounced worldly pursuits. Usually, there is a formal ceremony conducted by the *guru* or teacher after which *sannyasa* is formally conferred. The

---

* *'Bhikku'* is derived from *'bhikshu'*, a Sanskrit word that means 'one who lives on alms' or 'the ascetic'.

usual practice is to wear ochre-coloured robes.* However, details of external appearance such as clothes and shaven head are often not rigorously followed or imposed.

In the Gita, the words *sannyasi* and *yogi* are used frequently. Some of the descriptions include passages such as:

अनाश्रितः कर्मफलं कार्यं कर्म करोति यः |
स संन्यासी च योगी च न निरग्निर्न चाक्रियः ||

Anasritah karmaphalam karyam karma karoti yah; sah samnyasi cha yogi, na niragnir na cha akriyah. (6.1)

[He who does allotted work without seeking its fruits, he is the *sannyasi*, he is the *yogi*. Not those who give up *agni,* fire and work.]

Here, 'agni' refers to the tradition where the *sannyasi* gives up performing (Vedic) rituals with fire or *agni* with an eye on its worldly results. The emphasis is on inner renunciation rather than on giving up rituals or work. The following verse goes on to say:

यं संन्यासमिति प्राहुर्योगं तं विद्धि पाण्डव |
न ह्यसंन्यस्तसङ्कल्पो योगी भवति कश्चन ||

---

* Buddhists, Christians and one sect of Jain monks (*Svetambara*) and nuns also have distinctively coloured or white robes.

Yam sannyasam iti prahur yogam tam viddhi Pandava,
na-hya-sannyasasta sankalpo yogi bhavati kaschana. (6.2)

[What they call *sannyasa*, know O Pandava (Arjuna)!
No one becomes a *yogi* without giving up worldly
desires.]

Though '*sankalpa*' is usually translated as 'worldly desires',
it literally means 'a firm intention for achieving some
objective'. Since all objectives are irrelevant to realizing the
Self, we should give up all such intentions. However, we
still continue to do the work that comes naturally to us, as
mentioned in the previous verse. The Gita also says, '*Jneyah
sa nitya sannyasi, yo na dvesti na kankshati*', which can be
translated as 'Know him as the *sannyasi* who neither hates
nor desires.' The emphasis is on renunciation of worldly
desires for the *sannyasi* and the *yogi*. The mind which is
constantly attracted to other pursuits will not easily fix
itself on God or Brahman.

A related word is '*tyaga*' which also means 'renunciation'
or 'giving up'. The Gita refers to this repeatedly, for
instance, in such phrases as '*sangam tyaktva phalam
chaiva*' ('giving up attachment and the fruits of action')
and '*sarvadharman pari-tyajya*' ('giving up all *dharmas*').
The phrase '*sangam tyaktva*' or 'giving up attachment' is
used repeatedly, as is '*karma phalam tyaktva*' or 'giving
up the fruits of action'. The Kaivalya and Mahanarayano

Upanishads have a famous verse that says '*tyagenaika amritatva*', where '*tyagena*' means 'by renunciation' and '*eika amritatva*' means 'alone do you attain Immortality'. *Tyaga* thus means simply giving up whereas *sannyasa* refers to the more formal and complete renunciation of all worldly pursuits.[6]

The word '*mantra*' is used often in the scriptures. The definition of '*mantra*' is sometimes given as '*Mananat trayate iti mantra*' or 'That which by constant thinking or reflection protects the mind is *mantra*'. It implies the constant reflection on a sacred syllable that protects the mind and eventually leads to realization or illumination. *Mantras* are believed to have spiritual power. The *mantra* 'Om' is used repeatedly in the Upanishads as well as in the Bhagavad Gita and the Brahma Sutras. Some well-known *mantras* include the twenty-four syllable Gayatri Mantra in the Vedas and shorter ones such as '*Om Namah Sivay*' and '*Om Namo Narayanaya*'. In fact, there is a whole esoteric science behind *mantras* which is usually handed down in person from teacher to disciple. The idea is that only those who are illumined have the authority to pass on the sacred and powerful *mantra* to the disciple. The *mantra* acquires real power only when it has been transmitted from the teacher to the disciple. However, some *mantras* such as 'Om' are intrinsically powerful.

The idea of sound or the Sacred Word is important. The Bible says, 'In the beginning was the Word and the

Word was with God, and the Word was God.' One such sacred word is 'Amen', which sounds similar to 'Om'. In Islam and Judaism, the word 'Amin' is sometimes used. As mentioned earlier, the Upanishads and the Bhagavad Gita repeatedly say that the sound symbol 'Om' is Brahman, the manifest and the unmanifest universe. It is considered that some word symbols or *mantras* possess spiritual power. In Hinduism, there are many *mantras*. Some are available in the texts while others are passed down from teacher to student, from *guru* to *shishya*. It is said that a *mantra* from an enlightened *guru* has special power and can hasten the aspirant's journey on the spiritual path.

Closely related to the concept of *mantra* is that of '*japa*' which refers to the repetition of the mantra.* Such repetition is said to confer material, physical, psychological, mental, emotional and spiritual benefits. One method is to sit quietly and repeat the *mantra*, concentrating on the meaning of the *mantra*. It is said that this helps to make the mind calm and focused, and it is also one of the steps to meditation. The Patanjali Yoga Sutras use the term 'tadarthabhāvanam', referring to japa or the repetition of the mantra, paying attention to its meaning. The Bhagavad

---

* Repetition of sacred *mantras* or syllables is there in Buddhism, Christianity (where the rosary is used to repeat sacred words) and Islam (e.g., *Misbah* or *Tasbih*).

Gita says 'Yajna naam japa yagnosmi', or 'Among the yajnas (or sacrifices), I am japa.'

At the same time, the motivation or purpose of doing japa should be constantly examined. Japa done for a material or worldly purpose or with a lurking desire for something leads the mind astray, even though it may lead to the fulfilment of that objective. However, if performed for a spiritual purpose, japa enables spiritual progress or even illumination. Japa is not, however, the only path to spiritual growth. There are other methods that can be used in the spiritual life.

'*Yajna*' is another term often used in the Vedas and later scriptures. It is usually translated as 'sacrifice'. However, it has some connotations or meanings that are distinct. It is used in the Vedas and is associated with *agni* or fire sacrifice. But what is that sacrifice? It is invoking the higher powers or deities externally through the performance of rituals and the chanting of sacred *mantras* or syllables and also invoking these powers within oneself through that sacrifice. Chandrasekhara Saraswati, the respected erstwhile head of the Kanchi Math or Monastery says 'Yajna involves the performance of the prescribed rituals with the aid of Fire or *Agni,* to the accompaniment of Veda mantras.'[7] It is conducted with faith and concentration.

The word '*yajna*' is also used in a variety of contexts in the scriptures. In the Bhagavad Gita, it is used very frequently. It says '*Yajnanarthat karmano*' ('Do the work as a *yajna* or sacrifice'), '*Yajñāh karma-samudbhavaḥ*' ('*Yajna* comes from, or is born of, work') and '*Yajñāyācharataḥ karma*' ('Perform the work as a *yajna*'). In another verse the Gita uses the word *yajna* repeatedly

द्रव्ययज्ञास्तपोयज्ञा योगयज्ञास्तथापरे |
स्वाध्यायज्ञानयज्ञाश्च यतय: संशितव्रता: ||

Dravya-yajñās tapo-yajñā yoga-yajñās tathāpare
swādhyāya-jñāna-yajñāsh cha yatayaḥ sanśhita-vratāḥ.
(4.28)

[Some offer their wealth as sacrifice (*yajna*), while others offer *tapa* or austerities as *yajna*. Some offer yogic practices as *yajna*, some study the scriptures and offer knowledge as sacrifice while observing strict vows.]

Here, wealth, austerity, yogic practices, study, knowledge and austerity can all be offered as *yajna*. The word 'sacrifice' as understood in English conveys only a part of the meaning.

Any activity for a larger social or political purpose is also called *yajna* and there are many references in the Vedas to the *Ashvamedhayajna* and the *Rajasuyayajna*, sacrifices or rituals conducted by emperors and kings. The word '*yajna*' thus becomes difficult to define precisely in the English language. *Yajna* takes many forms and is an offering of one's effort, knowledge, work, austerity and mind to God or Brahman. It is understood that *yajna* done properly not only leads to the fulfilment of the objective one seeks, but also purifies the inner being of the individual.

Related to this is the idea of '*tapas*', which literally means 'heat' or 'burning'. It refers to the austerity and efforts made by the spiritual aspirant or devotee towards the objective. It also implies focusing the mind constantly, sometimes disregarding bodily and mental difficulties. Some practice bodily austerity, although that is discouraged by other texts. *Tapas* also includes discipline, moderation in speech, eating and sleeping and controlling the mind. *Tapasya* is the act of doing *tapas*. It is generally understood that the spiritual aspirant has to make efforts through *tapas*. Usually, the aspirant does whatever his temperament prompts from within, sometimes with the guidance of a teacher or *guru*. A popular phrase is '*japa-tapa*' or '*jap-tap*', meaning 'doing *japa* as *tapas*' or 'doing *japa* and *tapas*'.

'*Samskara*' has at least two meanings. In the Vedic context, it refers to life-stage *samskaras* or rituals, including marriage, the naming of a child, the first feeding ceremony, the initiation into student life and so on. In a broader sense, '*samskara*' refers to the impressions in the mind. All actions, reactions, thoughts, dreams, emotions and experiences create impressions or *samskaras* in the mind. Some are known to the individual and are called conscious, but most are subconscious and unconscious. These impressions define our individuality and character and make us act in ways that sometimes we are ourselves surprised by. However, the *jiva* can create new *samskaras*. Good actions create good *samskaras*. The mind can be controlled by creating good *samskaras* and by weakening the bad ones, eventually purifying the mind of all *samskaras*, both good and bad, and hence knowing the Truth and becoming illumined.[*]

'*Karma*' is another term that is used very often in the scriptures, from the Vedas and the Upanishads to later commentaries and texts. In the Vedic texts, it usually means the Vedic *karmas* or rituals, and the phrase 'Vedic *karmas*' is still in use. The first two parts of the Vedas are also known as the Karma Kanda (or ritual portion). Vedic *karmas* confer benefits such as health, wealth, prosperity, success, mental peace and purification. However, simply by themselves they cannot lead to the highest realization. They are thus classified as '*karma*' as opposed to '*jnana*' or knowledge which leads to realization. Traditionally, the *sannyasi* gives up the Vedic *karmas* and rituals as well as his caste.

The word '*karma*' has at least two other meanings. At one level, it simply means 'work' or 'action'. For instance,

---

[*] A similar concept is there in the Bible when Christ says to someone, 'Leave there thy gift before the altar, and go thy way; first be reconciled with thy brother. And then offer thy gift' (Mathew 5.24). The negative *samskara* of conflict with someone bothers the worshipper. God cannot accept such an offering. In Hinduism, it is said that the negative *samskaras* have to be removed or reconciled.

the Isa Upanishad uses the phrases '*Kurvann eveha karmāṇi*' or 'By doing works or action alone' and '*Na karma lipyate nare*', which means that action (done with the consciousness of the Lord who permeates the universe) does not bind man. Even in later texts such as the Bhagavad Gita, '*karma*' refers to action. At another level, '*karma*' also implies the well-known law of cause and effect that action produces on us. This is explained in the Bhagavad Gita. The effect of *karma* ordinarily binds us because it sets up the chain of cause and effect, each action leading to an effect which in turn leads to further action. However, action which is performed with the right attitude—that is, by giving up or renouncing the fruits of action—does not bind us. *Karma* refers to the fruits of action such as pleasure, disgust, victory, defeat, reward and punishment which create impressions in the mind. These impressions lead to further action for pleasure, victory, reward and so on. Even the avoidance of unpleasant consequences due to memories of disgust, failure and punishment is considered an action. When the fruits of action are given up and action is performed with detachment as a duty or as something that needs to be done, it does not create deep impressions in the mind. This breaks the chain of further action and eventually makes us free.

Sometimes, *karma* also refers to the sum total of all actions done by an individual. In popular usage, *karma* is occasionally used to mean 'fate', or the sheer weight of past actions that determine an individual's experiences in the present. If that is very powerful or causes suffering, popularly people say 'my *karma*' or fate. But this is not the right meaning as obtained from the scriptures. Some scholar-saints have insisted that *karma* is not a fatalistic theory at all but is, in fact, quite the opposite. If our past actions have brought us to this state at present, then our current and future actions too can create a better state.

'*Jiva*' is another term that is often used and refers to the individual soul. It usually denotes the ordinary individual who has not yet attained enlightenment and is ignorant of the Atman within.

Conclusions

Some of the important concepts and terms from Hinduism have been presented in this chapter. After the Vedas, various philosophical treatises, commentaries and other texts were written. The terms discussed here help us to understand these later texts. A few of the earlier terms used in the Vedas and Upanishads, such as 'Brahman', 'Atman' and 'Purusha' were discussed in the earlier chapters. In this chapter, the idea of God, the *avatar*, and terms such as '*yajna*', '*tapas*', '*mantra*', '*japa*', '*tapas*', '*karma*', '*samskara*' and '*jiva*' have been discussed. It is sometimes difficult to precisely define these terms, and the scriptures also use them in different contexts with different meanings. Scholars and commentators also interpret these terms differently. Popular notions sometimes differ from scholarly ones. However, there is always a broad sense and an underlying meaning which can be discerned. The most widely accepted meanings have been presented here.

4

THE SIX DARSANAS OR PHILOSOPHIES

This chapter is about the Shat Darsanas, the Six Darsanas or Philosophies that are considered to be a part of the sacred texts. Unlike the Vedas and Upanishads, they are not regarded as revelations. They use reason and assumptions or axioms to establish their philosophies and address fundamental questions such as what is the basic ground of existence? What is reality? Does reality have a form or is it formless? What is the nature of matter, life and spirit? What is the destiny of the individual? Does the soul exist? If it does, then what is its essential nature? Is there any purpose to all this?

The root word of '*darsana*' is '*drs*', which means 'to see'. In this context, '*darsana*' refers to seeing or envisioning the truth or philosophy. In other contexts, '*darsana*' refers to the sighting of God, an idol or a holy person.

The Six Philosophies are called '*astika*', meaning 'those that accept the primacy of the Vedas'. Other philosophies such as the Charvaka (popularly known as materialism),

Buddhism and Jainism that do not accept the Vedas are called *nastika*.* The term 'philosophy' is not an accurate translation of '*darsana*' which sometimes give teachings for attaining the end goal of the philosophy. For instance, some of the darsanas give indications on how to attain *nirvana* or liberation.

The Six Darsanas are Nyaya, Vaiseshika, Sankhya, Yoga, Purva Mimamsa and Uttara Mimamsa. The Uttara Mimamsa is sometimes referred to as Vedanta, which is why the term '*mimamsa*' by itself is usually taken to mean the Purva Mimamsa. Some of the *astika* philosophies are also either agnostic or atheistic. As one of the Six Darsanas, Yoga does not refer to the popular notion of physical exercises and deep breathing. It is a major spiritual text that discusses the union of the individual soul with the Divine. The Vedanta or Brahma Sutras are given the highest status among the Six Darsanas. The *prasthana traya*—the first three sacred texts—include it, the other two being the Vedas and the Bhagavad Gita.

Later philosophies which arose during the medieval period, in particular the Advaita, Visishtadvaita, Dvaita, Dvaita-Advaita, Shuddhadvaita and Achintya Bheda Abheda, are not part of the orthodox list of sacred texts. However, they are also revered by their adherents today.

---

* Today, *astika* also means belief in God and *nastika* means atheism. However, this is problematic in this context because Purva Mimamsa is classified as *astika* even though it negates the role of God.

In fact, they may have more adherents today than some of the ancient *darsanas* even though they emerged several centuries later. We will describe them in a later chapter.

These Six Darsanas were not static and, over the course of centuries, additional texts and commentaries were written. Although scholars differ in their interpretations of these texts, there are some essential points on which they agree. First, the supremacy of the Vedas is accepted by all. Another point of agreement is about the existence of a non-material Soul, variously called the Atman or Purusha. It refers to the existence of Consciousness.

Four of these *darsanas*—Nyaya, Vaiseshika, Sankhya and Yoga—do not refer directly to the Vedas to establish their philosophy. However, all of them accept the Vedas as the ultimate authority. For instance, one of the means of knowledge is called the '*sabda pramana*', which can be translated as 'the word ("*sabda*") is a means of obtaining knowledge'. Often, this is interpreted to mean the word of the Vedas. Other scholars say that '*sabda*' refers to the word of the '*apta*' or the knowledgeable individual. In modern terms, most of us accept the Theory of Relativity because everyone says that Einstein was a great scientist, and other scientists say his theory is correct, but few people actually read the theory and still fewer understand it. In the same way, the ancient *darsanas* say that *sabda* is a valid means of knowledge.

The differences between the *darsanas* are about the ultimate destiny of the Soul, the concept of God, the relationship between the individual and God, the means of reaching the goal of life and the relationship between the universe, the individual and God or the Ultimate Reality. God, in particular, is conceptualized in various ways. For instance, God is a manifestation of the Supreme Brahman and is both omnipotent and omniscient. As the Creator of the Universe, God can also have attributes. He can be the efficient cause of the universe, like the potter who creates a clay pot, and He can also be the material cause of the universe, like the spider which creates its own web. God bestows the fruits of action on human beings based on the laws of *karma*, cause and effect, action and reaction. However, the *darsanas* either accept or reject one or more of these concepts of God. But if God exists, then it is full of Consciousness. Sometimes, the differences between these philosophies are so stark that some later commentaries negate them and establish their own point of view.

Some philosophies sometimes accept the logic or methodology of another *darsana* while differing in other ways. For instance, although the logical basis of Nyaya and Vaiseshika is accepted by other *darsanas*, their conclusions are not always accepted. For instance, the Sankhya tenet of a Soul or Purusha is accepted by other philosophies as well as the Bhagavad Gita. However, Sankhya says there are separate Purusha in each individual, whereas the other philosophies say there is only one Purusha, Atman or Brahman that is manifested in different living beings. The psychology of Sankhya is also largely accepted by other philosophies although their conclusions differ. However, all the Six Darsanas are accepted as sacred texts and the differences between them are usually attributed to different ways of experiencing and understanding reality. At an individual level, each is free to accept or reject one or more of the philosophies.

All of them start off with a very logical foundation. They address the question of what is a valid means of knowledge? What is knowledge or Truth itself. The *darsanas* also use the term '*pramana*' which refers to the means of obtaining accurate and valid knowledge. In popular usage, this has now come to mean 'proof'. They describe the basis of *pramana* and then proceed to establish their philosophies.

Each of these *darsanas*, together with its various original *sutras*, commentaries and later texts, goes in to great detail and subtle arguments. Although a full grasp of each philosophy would require long and dedicated study, a brief overview of the essentials is given here.

Nyaya

'Nyaya' in Sanskrit literally means 'rule' or 'method of reasoning'.[*] It is based on logic and realism. In philosophical

---

[*] In modern language, '*nyaya*' is used variously as the law, as something that is just or fair. The presumption is that it is based on reason.

terms, 'realism' means to accept what we see, what we experience through our senses. In Nyaya, the world is real and exists independent of the mind. The original *sutra* or text was most likely composed in the 4th century BCE by Gautama (not to be confused with Gautama Buddha). Several commentaries were written on it over the centuries, right up to about 1650 CE.

Nyaya uses four *pramanas*, which are essentially bases or valid means of knowing the Truth. The first is known as *pratyaksha* or direct experience through the senses.* The second is *anumana* or inference or logical deduction. For instance, the presence of smoke is used to infer the existence of fire, because there can be no smoke without fire. Logic is one of the principal means of acquiring knowledge. The third *pramana* is known as *upamana* or comparison. For instance, someone who has not seen a wild cow is told by another that it resides in the forest. When this individual later sees such an animal in the forest, they conclude that it is a wild cow. The fourth *pramana* is *sabda*. Literally, '*sabda*' means 'word', which comes from a trustworthy source. Although this is usually interpreted as the word of

---

* For some scholars, '*pratyaksha*' later also came to mean direct experience of God or higher states of consciousness. In the Nyaya, however, *pratyaksha* refers to knowledge gained through the senses. Later Nyaya commentators also included direct perception going beyond sense perception.

the Vedas, it also includes the word or testimony of the worthy person, the *apta* Purusha.

This begs the question: what is valid knowledge? It is whether the concept or idea formed in the mind corresponds to reality. How can we ever know that? Nyaya accepts this difficulty and says that the test of truth is whether it can be repeated and practiced, or whether it leads to useful action. Truth is known in this sense through its utility.

Nyaya—or *tarka sastra*, as it also called—has an elaborate system of logic. It goes on to describe sixteen categories of the techniques of reasoning. These include doubting, arguing constructively or destructively, specious argumentation, attacking vulnerable points in an opponent's argument, using established facts and so on. Later Nyaya commentaries even seek to prove the existence of God. It uses well-known arguments used even today—the world must have come from somewhere; there is order in the universe; the universe is not chaotic; there exists a moral order; and no one has ever proved that God does not exist.

God is non-material and is Spirit. However, God is also the Prime Mover, the One who creates, protects, destroys and re-creates the universe. Like the Soul, God is eternal but is always conscious. The individual Soul is not always conscious and does not have the power to create the universe. Like two other *darsanas*, Vaiseshika and Sankhya, Nyaya says there are many souls. Each soul goes through cycles of birth and death based on its *karma*. It is released when it gains knowledge. This release is marked by the total absence of pain. Nyaya takes the view that defining liberation as happiness is not correct since it always alternates with sorrow or pain.

One principal contribution of Nyaya is the use of logic. Its conclusions and philosophy may not have been accepted by other schools of thought, but use of logic has prevailed. This has been used by all *darsanas* and later philosophies right down to the present day.

Vaiseshika

The word '*vaiseshika*' literally means 'specific' or 'particular'. One of the distinctive features of Vaiseshika is the classification into categories. One of them is 'particularity' or '*visesa*'. The original *sutra* is Kanada's Vaiseshika Sutra. It was composed around the same time as Nyaya, perhaps a bit earlier. Vaiseshika also uses logic and has similar metaphysical theories about the universe and God. Vaiseshika and Nyaya became tied to each other. Later commentaries use concepts from both the original texts.

The theory of knowledge according to Vaiseshika has only two *pramanas—pratyaksha* or perception and *anumana* or logic and reasoning. Later texts argue that that the other two *pramanas* of Nyaya—comparison and testimony of authority—are based on logical inference and thus there is no need to include them separately.

Vaiseshika goes into the question of all that can be known. A category or '*padartha*' is something that can be known ('*jneya*'), validly cognized ('*prameya*') and properly denoted or described ('*abhideya*'). At first, only six categories were present, with a seventh being added later. The six categories are substance or '*dravya*', quality or '*guna*', activity or '*karma*', the general or '*samanya*', the particular or '*visesa*' and the inherent or inseparable relationship between two substances or '*samavaya*'. Later, non-existence or '*abhava*' was added. Thus, anything can be known through these categories. This categorization is perhaps one of the most distinctive features of Vaiseshika.

The physical world can ultimately be resolved into atoms beyond which matter cannot be broken down. These atoms give rise to things by combining in different ways. It uses logic to establish this premise. Its metaphysics about the ultimate destiny of the soul is similar to Nyaya. According to Vaiseshika, there exist many souls and they are liberated after repeated cycles of birth and death according to their *karma* by gaining knowledge. Liberation is complete absence of pain just as it is in Nyaya.

Sankhya

Sankhya is an important *darsana* as it has influenced Hindu psychology, especially when applied to spiritual seekers. For instance, the Bhagavad Gita has a chapter entitled 'Sankhya Yoga'. The Patanjali Yoga Sutras use the basic ideas of Sankhya regarding the ego, the mind and the impressions that are buried in it. There are references in the Vedas to ideas similar to those in Sankhya. Sankhya had a major influence on later philosophies and some of its basic precepts were accepted by them. Today, spiritual seekers may not study the Sankhya, but they do study the later texts that are influenced by it.

Sankhya is usually attributed to the sage, Kapila. The word 'sankhya' literally means 'to count or enumerate'. The original Sankhya (alternately spelled as 'Samkhya') Sutras were written by Kapila but were lost. The Sankhya Karika or commentary was written by Ishwarakrishna much later, sometime around 350 CE. By this time, Buddhism and Jainism were established, and some ideas in Sankhya are similar to their tenets.

Briefly, the Sankhya Karika says that human beings are subject to various miseries which leads to the desire to be free of them. One of the means to be free of such misery is to follow what the Vedas say, but study of the Vedas alone is not sufficient. A knowledge of the universe around us is the first step to liberation. Distinct from this universe is the Purusha, which is present in every human being. These two, Purusha and Prakriti (Nature) are the 'mula' or the very bases of reality. Knowledge is gained through perception, inference or reason and valid testimony.

Knowledge obtained merely through the senses is limited and not sufficient. For acquiring knowledge beyond the senses, either revelation or the valid testimony of those who possess that knowledge is required. It then says that everything in the universe is based on cause and effect. These are perceived through the attributes of *sattva*, *rajas* and *tamas*. This well-known tripartite classification is not only used in later philosophies but is also prevalent today. '*Sattva*' denotes a mind that is calm, balanced, in equilibrium and bright; '*rajas*' denotes the qualities of energy, passion and activity; and '*tamas*' denotes dullness, lethargy and laziness. We perceive Nature around us using our mind which has all the qualities of *sattva*, *rajas* and *tamas* in varying degrees at various times. 'Nature' here implies everything that is not consciousness, including the physical, mental, emotional and subtle elements like dreams and tendencies arising out of the impressions in the subconscious mind. Since minds are different, what is perceived is also different.

All this, whether the physical or mental universe rests on the Unmanifest. It implies that as we resolve everything we observe, which is an effect, into its cause, and each cause into its cause and so on, it leads to an ultimate source from which everything we observe and experience arises which is the Unmanifest. The Unmanifest is also called 'Mahat', which is the potential form from which everything in the universe evolves.* Then it says that since there is an observer and experiencer, there exists a separate reality called the Purusha. This Purusha is Consciousness and different from Prakriti. Each individual has a distinct Purusha, even though all are essentially identical. Other philosophies say that there is only one Purusha, only One Consciousness that manifests itself in different living beings.

The '*jiva*' or individual is born of the union of Purusha and Prakriti. It leads to the birth of 'Buddhi' or intelligence and 'Ahamkara' or ego. Everything other than consciousness or Purusha is considered to be a part of Prakriti, including matter, energy and even internal things such as ego, emotions and thoughts.

Sankhya describes twenty-four *tattvas* or principles. Purusha is pure Consciousness and causeless, and is not counted as a principle or *tattva*. The first *tattva* is Prakriti, which is also causeless and goes on to describe how evolution takes place. The juxtaposition of Purusha and Prakriti gives rise to Mahat or the entire universe in its potential form. This forms the basis from which everything evolves. This Mahat is latent and evolves into the world as we see it. In its individual form, this juxtaposition first leads to Buddhi, usually translated as intelligence and discrimination. Mahat (the universal aspect) or Buddhi

---

* Some scholars say that Mahat is a concept of God. Others disagree, and say that Sankhya is agnostic or even atheistic.

(individual aspect) is the second *tattva*. Subsequently, the Ahamkara or ego evolves and is regarded as the third *tattva*. Ahamkara refers to the identification of the *jiva* or individual with the body thoughts and emotions and not merely to the assertion of individuality or ego. Manas or mind constitutes the fourth *tattva*.

Sankhya says explicitly that Prakriti exists for the individual Purusha to gain experience and has no other purpose. Purusha in a way forgets its true nature when united with Prakriti and identifies with the Ahamkara and Buddhi.[*] Liberation is achieved when the Purusha realizes its own true nature.

Sankhya also describes the universe as we experience it, exploring questions of how we gain knowledge and how we perform action. It describes how the impressions of knowledge and action are stored in us. It also describes the external universe. The five instruments of knowledge are called *jnanendriyas*, the five instruments of action are the *karmendriyas* and the means by which impressions are stored in human beings are the five *tanmatras*. The external world is described though five *panchabhutas*.

The instruments to perceive Prakriti include the five *jnanendriyas* or sense organs and the five *karmendriyas*.[1]

---

[*] A few centuries later, the great Advaitic philosopher Adi Sankara composed a famous song called '*Nirvana Satakam*' or 'the Song of Nirvana'. The opening stanza says, 'I am not the mind, intelligence, ego or the impressions in the mind, I am pure Consciousness.'

Sankhya says that they emerge from the Ahamkara. Together with the mind, they are referred to as the eleven instruments. The *'jnanendriyas'* literally mean 'organs of knowledge'. They are the ear, eye, tongue, skin and nose. The *'karmendriyas'* are 'instruments of action'. They are the organs of speech, hands, feet, excretion and reproduction. The eleven instruments are said to emerge from *sattva*. The mind or Manas has the nature of both the sense organs and the organs of action. The jnanendriyas are only for observation, the karmendriyas are for action. The three *tattvas* of intelligence, ego and mind are called the *'antahkarana'* ('internal') while the *jnanendriyas* and *karmendriyas* are called *'bahyam'* ('external'). These ten *indriyas* together with Prakriti or external Nature are meant for the Purusha to gain experience and, through experience, liberation.

There are also five *panchabhutas* which are gross and emerge from *tamas*. These include space, air, fire, water and earth, and they emerge from *tamas* because they are inert. It is interesting to note that the five senses are linked to how we perceive the world. Hearing, touch, vision, taste and smell provide knowledge that we receive from the five senses. The five *panchabhutas* are also perceived by these senses. Space is perceived only by hearing (as understood when Sankhya was composed), air by hearing and touch, fire by hearing, touch and vision, water by all the senses except smell and, finally, earth by all the five senses.

There are also five *tanmatras* or subtle impressions. '*Tanmatras*' refer to the impressions created in the mind by observing and experiencing things around us and include sound, form, taste, touch and smell. We can experience these in subtle form even without external stimuli through imagination, thought and dream.* The *tanmatras* in subtle form are the cause of the experiences we have with the grosser sense organs and organs of action. The basic insight in Sankhya is that actions and impressions gathered by the senses are 'stored' in the mind in the form of *tanmatras* and memory.

This brings the total number of *tattvas* to twenty-four. The first four are Prakriti, Mahat/Buddhi, Ahamkara and Manas. Then there are the five each of *jnanendriyas*, *karmendriyas*, *tanmatras* and *panchabhutas*. In Sankhya, these describe the universe as we experience it. Modern physics and science usually have a very different understanding of the universe based on reason and information gathered by various instruments. However, if we ask how do we perceive and experience the universe (both external and internal), Sankhya provides an answer that may be valid even today.

The later *darsanas* or philosophies largely accept this characterization of the individual into twenty-four *tattvas*

---

* The philosophy of Yoga contains the idea of '*chitta*' or 'mind stuff' which is the seat of memory. *Tanmatras* are in a sense stored in memory, and can be conscious, subconscious and even unconscious.

together with the influence of the three *gunas* or qualities of *sattva*, *rajas* and *tamas*. However, they differ in their conclusions, a point to which we will return later.

Sankhya says that Buddhi is the primary instrument for freeing the Purusha from its entanglement with Prakriti and the *tattvas*. Here, 'Buddhi' refers not only to intelligence as popularly understood but also to the faculty of discrimination. Buddhi tells the mind what is good, what is not, what is permanent and what is temporary.[*]

Sankhya says that the subtle body constituted by the *tanmatras* exists beyond death while the gross body born of parents is short-lived. The subtle body is created in the beginning with Mahat and is dissolved either when creation is dissolved or when the individual is liberated. This subtle body takes birth again and again, impelled by the purpose of Purusha which is to ultimately free itself while going through various experiences. In a sense, this is what is meant by the idea of reincarnation.

Practising virtue, avoiding vice, keeping the mind calm and sticking to the truth are all aids to attaining freedom. There is a very powerful statement in Sankhya which says that once the Purusha has seen Prakriti for what it really is, it is no longer attached to it. In poetic language, Sankhya also says that Prakriti, knowing that is has been

---

[*] Later texts sometimes use the specific term '*viveka*' to denote the faculty of discrimination.

observed, ceases to function for that individual. This leads to *samyak* jnana* or complete knowledge. This leads to liberation which includes absence of misery, presence of peace and joy and freedom from rebirth. The term used is '*kaivalya*'. *Nirvana*, *moksha* and *mukti* all refer to the same thing as *kaivalya*.

Sankhya perhaps derived its name from the fact that it 'enumerates' or 'counts' the twenty-four *tattvas* through which we experience the world. The Sankhya Karika by itself is completely silent on God, neither refuting nor accepting its existence. Sankhya's categorization of Soul and matter, together with the three *gunas* of *sattva*, *rajas* and *tamas*, is accepted by various other texts including the Bhagavad Gita and later philosophies. Sankhya explicitly refers to reincarnation and freedom from rebirth. Reincarnation is an important aspect of the Six Darsanas as well as other religions including Buddhism, Jainism and Sikhism. The Yoga Sutras, another of the Six Darsanas, uses the ideas in Sankhya to show a path to liberation. It uses the psychology that emerges from the concepts of the Buddhi, ego and mind as well as the subtle impressions or *tanmatras*. The idea that perfect knowledge leads to *kaivalya* or liberation is also present in other scriptures and texts, notably the Advaita philosophy of Adi Sankara.

---

* The term '*samyak*' is repeatedly used in the Eightfold Path outlined by the Buddha.

Yoga

As a *darsana* or philosophy, Yoga is derived from the root word '*yuj*' which means 'to yoke'. It refers to the union of the individual soul with the Divine. Yoga is not philosophical or metaphysical but is a method of reaching the goal of life. It accepts some of the ideas of Sankhya. The principal text is considered to be the Yoga Sutras of Patanjali composed in the 5th or 6th century CE. However, the basic ideas of Yoga existed long before that and references can be found in the Upanishads and the Bhagavad Gita. Other names for Yoga include Dhyana Yoga (the Yoga of Meditation) and Raja Yoga (the Royal Yoga). Several commentaries on the Yoga Sutras were written later.

The primary method is mind control through concentration. Union with the Divine is not possible with an agitated or confused mind. The mind must first be calmed, and one method is concentration. The well-known aphorism '*Yoga chitta vritti nirodha*' in the second verse of the Yoga Sutras says, 'Yoga is the control of the modifications of the *chitta* or mind stuff'.* The word '*chitta*' refers to the mind, memory and, according to some, the storehouse of all conscious, subconscious and even unconscious impressions. These give rise to thoughts and impel action, creating constant fluctuations in the mind.

---

* Making the mind still is also referred to in the well-known Biblical statement 'Be still and know that I am God' (Psalm 46:10).

These impressions do not allow the Truth to be revealed. The verse gives the definition, the goal and the means for attaining Yoga. That stilling of the mind leads to revelation or *samadhi* and liberates the *jiva*.

Chapter 6 of the Bhagavad Gita is devoted to the Yoga of Meditation. Krishna talks about the means and the end result of this practice. Calming and stilling the mind through concentration is the principal means. It describes the state of mind of the *yogi* as similar to the light of a lamp that is steady in a windless place. Stilling the mind leads to its purification and brings permanent joy and bliss. The *yogi* is then ever satisfied and does not seek anything else. The student, Arjuna then says that the mind is impossible to control, more difficult to control than the wind. Krishna agrees and says that through repeated practice and detachment, the mind is eventually brought under control.

The Yoga Sutras go into much greater detail, explaining the principal obstacles to knowing the Truth. The latent tendencies in the *chitta* give rise to action, which leads to impressions which in turn, lead to action and thus the cycle continues. The individual knows no peace. Ignorance (*avidya*), erroneous identification with the body and mind (*asmita*), attachment (*raga*), aversion (*dvesa*) and clinging to life and dreading death are said to be the obstacles to Truth. Acknowledging the difficulty of overcoming them, the Sutras suggest the Ashtanga (literally, 'eight limbs') Yoga.

The first two—*yama* and *niyama*—are the ethical basis of Yoga. *Yama* consists of non-injury (*ahimsa*), truth (*satya*), non-stealing (*asteya*), celibacy (*brahmacharya*) and non-acceptance of gifts (*aparigraha*). These are linked to avoiding wrong actions. *Niyama* consists of purity (*saucha*), contentment (*santosha*), austerity (*tapas*), self-study (*svadhaya*) and surrender to God (*Ishwara pranidhana*). These are the teachings on right actions.

The next three steps—*asana*, *pranayama* and *pratyahara*—help one to discipline the body and mind and make it fit for attaining the state of *yoga* or union. However, the first two steps cannot be ignored. *Asana* is a posture that one can hold for a long time, and keep the body still. The spine must be straight.* The idea is that the body must not be a hindrance in the practice of meditation. '*Pranayama*' literally means 'control of *prana* or the life energy'. Its principal means is breath control. It was discovered that regular, steady breathing helps to calm the mind, and in fact the converse is also true, i.e., that a calm mind leads to steady breathing. '*Pratyahara*'

---

* It is assumed that for the consciousness to rise freely without hindrance, the spine has to be straight. The *yogic* power—also referred to sometimes as *Kundalini*—rises without hindrance when the spine is straight. In popular culture, *asanas* refer to various physical exercises that lead to better health. They are from a separate text called the *Hathayoga Pradeepika*. These physical exercises are not what the Yoga Sutras refer to as *asana*.

literally means 'control of *ahara*', which in this context means control of all that we imbibe through the mind and the senses. Some scholars give greater emphasis on the food we eat than to what we imbibe through the other senses.

The final three steps are *dharana*, *dhyana* and *samadhi*. '*Dharana*' means 'concentration'. *Dhyana* refers to the deepening of concentration and is often translated as 'meditation'. It is compared to the steady and silent flowing of oil—*taila dharavat*. By now a considerable degree of control over the thoughts has been achieved. This leads to calmness and, occasionally, to super-sensuous experiences, visions and hearing voices. It can also lead to *yogic* powers. Patanjali cautions the reader not to get swayed or diverted by these phenomena since running after sensory things and feeding the ego may lead to a fall and, occasionally, to degeneration.

The final stage is called *samadhi*, which can be literally translated as 'an equanimous mind'. More broadly, however, it refers to enlightenment. The mind becomes still, there is peace and bliss, and it transforms the individual. Having experienced this, the individual no longer has any interest in sensory and worldly pursuits. The Yoga Sutras describe two broad levels of *samadhi*. The first or lower one is called *samprajnata samadhi*. Here the tendencies in the mind have been silenced but not eradicated. It describes variations within this *samadhi* which eventually lead to *sananda samadhi* or the 'blissful *samadhi*'. Though the mind is stilled, there is an awareness of a separation between the knower and the object. This is not complete unity. Various stages are mentioned in *samprajnata samadhi*. Some other terms such as *savikalpa* ('with thought') or *sabija* ('with seed') *samadhi* are also used.

At a higher level is *asamprajnata samadhi* where the mind completely ceases to function. After going through the earlier stages, the *yogi* enters this state of awareness and this knowledge destroys all *samskaras* or impressions and tendencies latent in the mind, including the subconscious and unconscious ones. Consequently, these *samskaras* cannot sprout again and hence there is no rebirth. The *jiva* becomes free and goes beyond the cycle of birth and death, and becomes one with Brahman. This *samadhi* is also called *nirbija* ('without seed') or Nirvikalpa *samadhi* (without any thought, even the thought of being aware) or total unity with Brahman.

Yoga accepts God or Ishwara. Here, Ishwara refers to Omniscience, the Teacher of teachers. It does not refer explicitly to Ishwara's role as the Creator. Yoga accepts Sankhya regarding the separation of the soul and matter, soul and thoughts, and the classification into ego, mind and intelligence. It however says there is a God, about which Sankhya is agnostic

Of all the *darsanas*, the Yoga Sutras are used even today, and many study them and try to put their teachings into practice. Usually, the need for an adept teacher or *guru* is always emphasized before one practises this Yoga.

Purva Mimamsa

The earlier *darsanas* do not refer to the Vedas or the Upanishads. Although they accept them, they base their philosophy on reason and logic or, as in the case of the Yoga Sutras, on direct experience. But the Purva Mimamsa (or, simply, the Mimamsa) and Vedanta explicitly refer to passages in the Vedas to establish their philosophy. '*Purva*' means 'earlier' and refers to the earlier sections of the Vedas. The word '*mimamsa*' means 'an enquiry into truth'.

The sage Jaimini is the author of the Mimamsa which is said to be around 400 BCE. '*Mimamsa*' literally means 'logical enquiry'. It enquires into the Vedas to build its philosophy. There were several commentaries on this. The earliest was by Sabara. A later important commentary was by Kumarila Bhatta, a contemporary of Adi Sankara, in the 8th century CE. Prabhakara also wrote a commentary.

Mimamsa bases itself on the Karma Kanda or the first two parts of the Vedas, namely the Mantra Samhitas and the Brahmanas. Recall that samhitas are the *mantras* or sacred syllables and hymns while the Brahmanas provide injunctions on ritual practices as well as the meaning of these *mantras*. Mimamsa does not base itself on the latter two parts of the Vedas, that is, the Aranyakas and the Upanishads.

Mimamsa aims to show that the Vedas are supreme and that the rituals contained in the Vedas are the primary teachings. Later commentaries on the Purva Mimamsa accept all the *pramanas* of the other *darsanas*, including direct (*pratyaksha*), inference (*anumana*), comparison (*upamana*) and testimony of the word (*sabda*). It adds presumption or *arthapatti* and non cognition or *anupalabdhi* (non-cognition), However, it gives supreme status to *sabda* which, in this case, clearly refers to the Karma Kanda of the Vedas. According to the Mimamsa, *sabda* is the highest *pramana*. It uses its system of logic to establish that the Vedas are not by man (*apaurusheya*), that they are eternal (*nitya*), without beginning (*anaadi*) and infinite (*ananta*).

Mimamsa says that the relationship between the sound of a word and its meaning is such that it cannot be separated and in that sense, is eternal. However, this is true of all words. The Vedas are special because the order in which the words are arranged is not determined by any human or divine agent. Correct knowledge is also self-valid or self-evident and so are the Vedas. However, all other knowledge is defective since it originates from man. The knowledge in the Vedas is free from defect since it does not come from a human source. The Vedas also refer to that which is super-sensory.

Mimamsa says that the purpose of the Vedas is to teach *dharma* which, in this case, means religious duty. Injunctions about what should be done and what should be avoided constitute the Vedic *dharma*. One important aspect is its focus on Vedic rituals. These are required to be performed in the prescribed manner. The *nityakarmas* are rituals which should always be done. Although they confer no special benefit, not performing them leads to harm. Then there are the *samskaras* which are related to birth, marriage and death as well as rituals as *anna prasana* (the first feeding of the baby with solid food), *upanayana* (formal induction into student life through a ritual called the 'thread ceremony') and *samavartana* (graduating from the student life). These are also required to be done at the appropriate time in the prescribed manner. There also *kamya karmas* or rituals performed with desire. These include *karmas* for the birth of a son and for gaining a kingdom—the well-known Rajasuya and Ashvamedha *yajnas*. These were performed in both the Ramayana and the Mahabharata even though they were written centuries later. There are also *karmas* for the general welfare of society, for bringing rainfall and so on. *Kamya karmas* need not be done if there is no such desire.

Its position on the Upanishads is clear. The Upanishads are not injunctions about what needs to be done but are merely statements of fact. The purpose of the Vedas, however, is not to make factual statements but to guide human beings and tell them what to do. Even within the Karma Kanda, there are statements about Brahman but they do not provide any guide to action. Similarly, Mimamsa does not invoke God or even the Vedic deities. The Vedas are eternal and were not created by God. God is not required as a creator since the universe has always existed. God is also not required for bestowing the fruits of action, as they are determined by the Vedic *karmas*. Later commentaries tend to accept God.

The goal of life is to follow the Vedic *dharma* and reap the rewards accruing from it. Such reward includes the various higher levels of heaven described. Later commentators accepted *moksha* or liberation as a goal of life but insisted that achieving such *moksha* required a strict observance of the Vedic rituals.

The Bhagavad Gita says that those who follow the Vedic *karmas* ascend to heaven but have to be reborn. For liberation, they must follow the higher teachings. These views are more explicitly stated by Adi Sankara. Visishtadvaita and Dvaita follow Vedic rituals to a greater extent and enjoin the devotee or seeker to follow them.

There is an inherent tendency in man to seek wealth, prosperity and happiness, an impulse which is acknowledged and accepted by both the Vedic *karmas* and Mimamsa. Vedic rituals continue to be performed today, in particular during marriage and death. Elaborate rituals are also done on some occasions. Many Vedic *pandits* can chant the

Mantra Samhita of the Vedas, and in many religious and spiritual places, the Vedic *mantras* are chanted daily.

The *shanti mantras* which invoke peace are different from the Mantra Samhita, although they are very much in use even today and are also chanted regularly in various functions. Some of the well-known Vedic hymns such as the Purusha Suktam and the Rudram are also regularly chanted.*

Vedanta or Uttara Mimamsa

'*Uttara*' here refers to the latter section of the Vedas—the Upanishads. Uttara Mimamsa is better known as Vedanta, the 'end' or 'goal' of the Vedas. The major text is the Vedanta Sutras, also known as the Brahma Sutras or the Bhikshu† Sutras. The Vedanta Sutras are believed to have been composed around 400 BCE by Badarayana (who is thought by some to be the same as Veda Vyasa). Since there is a reference to the Brahma Sutras in the Bhagavad Gita, they are believed to predate the Gita although they postdate the Principal Upanishads.

The major departure of the Uttara Mimamsa is its emphasis on the Upanishads as the basis of Vedanta rather

---

* Other *mantras* such as the Vishnu Sahasranama, Lalita Sahasranama, Chandi or Devi Mahatmyam are not from the Vedas but from the Puranas and other texts.
† '*Bhikshu*' refers to mendicant monks.

than the Karma Kanda. Since Vedanta has dominated Hindu philosophy and has given rise to various later doctrines, it is discussed in the next chapter.

Summary

The Six Darsanas are based on reason and logic even though they accept the primacy of the Vedas. With the exception of the Yoga Sutras which offer a method of reaching the goal of life, they are philosophies and not revelations. There are differences among the philosophies. In practice, the earliest ones (such as the Nyaya and Vaiseshika) are studied only by scholars and have only indirectly influenced the practice of religion and spirituality today. Sankhya has far more influence on later philosophies, although such influence is also indirect. The entire psychological basis of the Yoga Sutras is derived from Sankhya. The Yoga Sutras are very much studied even today by serious spiritual seekers. The Purva Mimamsa with its exclusive focus on the Vedic rituals has perhaps only a few adherents today. However, Vedic rituals are still practised and there are many religious schools which teach Vedic chanting, performance of rituals and so on. Uttara Mimamsa or Vedanta is much more prevalent today, with people studying it and lectures, talks and books being devoted to the subject.

References

Swami Virupakshananda, *The Sankhya Karika of Isvara Krishna* (Chennai: Ramakrishna Math, 1995).

Swami Krishnananda, *The Teachings of the Bhagavadgita* (The Divine Life Society), chapters 3 and 5, https://www.swami-krishnananda.org/bhagavad/bhagavad_03.html; https://www.swami-krishnananda.org/phil-psy/phil-psy_05.html.

Swami Krishnananda, *Bhagavadgita*, chapter 5, https://www.swami-krishnananda.org/phil-psy/phil-psy_05.html. Cosmology according to Yoga and Sankhya, Swami Krishnananda, The Divine Life Society.

T.M.P. Mahadevan, *Outlines of Hinduism* (Mumbai: Chetana, 1999).

5

THE BRAHMA SUTRAS

The Brahma Sutras are also known as the Vedanta Sutras and the Bhikshu* Sutras (that is, *sutras* for monks or *sannyasis*). They provide a systematic and logical basis for Vedanta or the Upanishads. The Upanishads are 'revealed texts' and do not contain any well-developed philosophy. The Upanishadic verses are regarded as revelations of Truths 'seen' in higher states of consciousness. Although the Brahma Sutras are part of the Shat Darsanas, they occupy a special place in their own right. They form the basis of Uttara Mimamsa also called Vedanta.

The Brahma Sutra is one of the three most sacred texts—the *prasthana traya*—of Hinduism. '*Prasthana*' here means 'origin' or 'source'† and '*traya*' can be translated as

---

* '*Bhikshu*' literally means 'one who lives on alms'. Although the modern-day *sannyasi* is supported by society, the *sannyasi* of ancient times lived on alms.

† In everyday usage, '*prasthana*' means 'departure'. However, one of the meanings of the word is also 'origin' or 'source', which may be more apt here.

'three' or 'triad'. The three are the Upanishads, the Brahma Sutras and the Bhagavad Gita. It is generally accepted that the Brahma Sutras postdate the major Upanishads but predate the Bhagavad Gita. The Upanishads are called the *sruti prasthana*, meaning 'the text that was heard (in revelation)' and the *upadesa prasthana*, meaning 'the text that gives the teaching'. The Brahma Sutras are called the *sutra prasthana*, where 'a Sutra should be concise and unambiguous, give the essence of the arguments on a topic but at the same time deal with all aspects of the question, be free from repetition and is faultless'.[1] They are also occasionally referred to as the *nyaya prasthana*, meaning 'that which provides the logical basis of the Upanishads'. The Bhagavad Gita is sometimes called the *sadhana prasthana*, meaning 'that which explains how the teachings can be put into practice'.

According to one view, Veda Vyasa, who compiled the Vedas, is the same as Badarayana, who composed the Brahma Sutras. Another view is that the Brahma Sutras were composed earlier by Badarayana and were written down later by Vyasa.[*] The Gita refers to the Brahma

---

[*] Veda Vyasa is said to have compiled the Vedas and written the Brahma Sutras as well as the Mahabharata, which contains the Bhagavad Gita. Since these scriptures are separated by long periods of time, some people doubt whether Vyasa refers to the same person. Some consider that 'Vyasa' is a title given to a learned author of scriptures and, as such, it was applied to different people. Others, however, say

Sutras, but in turn the Brahma Sutras refer to the Gita indirectly. The general consensus today is that Vyasa wrote the Mahabharata, of which the Gita is a part, and also compiled the Brahma Sutras, adding some verses referring to the ideas in the Gita in the process.

Soon after the Upanishads, several philosophies arose, including the Nyaya, Vaiseshika and Sankhya,* each perhaps trying to prove that they were right. According to one count, there were sixty-two such schools. One of them—the Charvaka—is materialist and uses logic to establish its point of view. Possibly a need was felt to put the main ideas in Vedanta into a systematic philosophy, which was accomplished by the Brahma Sutras.

The Brahma Sutras is a relatively short text of only 555 verses. They are extremely concise and have short, terse phrases. The meaning of each *sutra* is often difficult to fully comprehend. Later, several commentaries or *bhashyas* were written by several people. The five most well-known commentaries are by Sankaracharya, Ramanujacharya, Madhavacharya, Nimbarkacharya and Vallabhacharya.

---

that Badarayana was the author of the Brahma Sutras and Vyasa later compiled it. Adi Sankara in his 8th-century commentary, refers to Badarayana but not to Vyasa. The problem of establishing the exact origin, history and authorship of some of the ancient texts is widely prevalent in Hinduism. However, the texts themselves have come down to the present day and are widely accepted as sacred.

* The Buddha found various philosophies being debated, including some that emphasized Vedic rituals.

Each of them used the Brahma Sutras as well as the Upanishads to establish different philosophies. These commentaries were necessary because the Brahma Sutras are so concise that the full meaning and interpretations of the *sutras* require explanations. The commentaries invariably went back to the Upanishads to establish what the *sutras* say. Later others wrote *tikas*, or further explanations of the *bhashyas*.

The Brahma Sutras also refer to earlier texts that evolved a similar philosophy from the Upanishadic texts. However, over time, the Brahma Sutras came to be accepted as the most authoritative.

The difficulty of precisely understanding what the Brahma Sutras say is largely because they are aphorisms that give very concise statements about what is written in the Upanishads. They do not, however, quote the Upanishads; instead, it is left to the commentator to choose the Upanishadic verse referred to by the relevant *sutra*. The meaning changes if the pauses in the text are modified slightly. There are two opposing points of view presented by the *Purvapaksha*, which provides a counter-argument and the *Siddhanta*, which establishes the Truth. There is no clear demarcation between the two, leaving it to the interpreter to decide which one is the Truth. Badarayana is also frequently silent about his own point of view and merely states the *sutras* and gives different points of view. For ease of exposition, we follow the Advaita interpretation of the Brahma Sutras. Later, we will discuss the interpretations of other Great Philosophies.

Glimpse into the Contents

A full study of the Brahma Sutras is required to understand the whole text. Ancient scholars have pointed out that a word by word understanding is not correct; instead, one has to arrive at the gist of the entire text. Another view argues it is not possible to say what the gist is a priori and that the text must be understood as it is.

The first *sutra* in the Brahma Sutras is:

अथातो ब्रह्माजिज्ञासा ॥

Athato Brahmajignasa
Atha—Now; *atah*—therefore; *brahmajijñāsā*—the inquiry into Brahman.

This is followed by:

जन्माद्यस्य यतः ॥

Janmādyasya yataḥ
[*Janmādi*—Origin (or birth); *asya*—of this (world); *yataḥ*—from which.]

This short *sutra* alone has extensive commentaries written on it by the great *acharyas* or teachers mentioned earlier. Although each commentator has a slightly different interpretation, the common consensus is that the enquiry into Brahman is required because it is the origin of everything.

The final *sutra* is:

अनावृत्तिः शब्दाद् अनावृत्तिः शब्दात्

Anavritti sabdaat, anavritti sabdaat

Literally, it means that 'there is no return on account of the word (of the scripture)'. This means there is no return to this world as *moksha* or liberation is achieved.

Scholars have pointed out that, in order to explain this verse, the great commentators have used different verses from the Upanishads. When it says '*sabdaat*', meaning 'as the scripture says', it does not say what part of scripture (that is, the Upanishads) is being referred to. Scholars have pointed out that the first and last verse of the 555 *sutras* show that the main purpose of the Brahma Sutras is to enquire into the nature of Brahman and show that for those who know Brahman, there is no return to this world by rebirth.

The text is divided into four chapters. The first chapter is called *Samanvaya Adhyaya* or the Study of Harmony and brings out the essential harmony or reconciliation of all the sayings in the Upanishads. It brings out the main purpose of the Upanishads, saying that:

तत् तु समन्वयात् ||

Tat tu samanvayāt
[*Tat*—That; *tu*—but; *samanvayāt*—there is harmony]

It indicates that the Upanishads have an essential harmony. Perhaps the title of this chapter is derived from this verse. The chapter takes several references and phrases in the Upanishads and says that they all pertain to Brahman alone. For example, the word '*prana*' which, properly understood, means 'energy' and 'life force', is stated in the Sutras as originating from Brahman. Similarly, matter, mind and various organs are all said to come from Brahman. The whole thrust of the chapter is to show that '*samanvay*', or harmony in all that the Upanishads say and to establish that it is about Brahman alone. It is the origin of everything, it is the original cause. It also briefly refutes theories which say that matter has always existed separate from Brahman. It refers to the Upanishads to establish this. Later commentators have referred to specific verses selected from the Upanishads to explain the meaning of the Sutras. However, the Dvaita interpretation states that living beings and matter are indeed distinct from Brahman.

The second chapter is called *Avirodha Adhayaya* or the Study without Contradiction. While the first chapter establishes that Brahman is the Primary Cause and the origin of everything, this chapter takes up other arguments that claim otherwise and refutes them. It says that matter does not have a separate origin. This refutes philosophies like Sankhya and Vaiseshika. The commentaries on the Brahma Sutras explain that they have been refuted, though the Sutras themselves do not refer by name to any of these two philosophies.

We need to recall that while these philosophies undoubtedly emphasized the reality and independence of matter, they also accepted the reality or experiences of man, that is, the thoughts and thought impressions. The second chapter of the Brahma Sutras also accepts the reality of the Self or Atman as distinct from matter. The major point of debate is whether this matter is eternally and fundamentally different from the Self. Later, it takes up purely materialist or nihilistic philosophies which state that things are ever-changing and that there is no such thing as the Self. All these other points of view are refuted and Brahman is established as real.

This chapter goes on to refute the philosophy which says that matter is separate from Brahman, that the sense organs are separate and that the enjoyer (or experiencer) is separate from that which is experienced. It also refutes the Smritis which explicitly say that the Shruti or Upanishads cannot be contradicted. The various *devas* (deities) mentioned also emanate from Brahman. It states that Brahman is not only the primal cause or the efficient cause of the universe but also its material cause. This means that Brahman is also matter. For instance, although the potter is the efficient cause of the pot he makes, the material cause is clay. However, a spider is not only the efficient cause of the web it creates but also the material cause as the web comes from the spider itself. This is only an analogy, but in a similar manner, Brahman alone 'Is' and is the efficient and material cause of the universe, and it is Brahman alone that pervades the universe. It refutes the argument that the world is differentiated and hence Brahman is also differentiated. It gives the examples of the dream state, where the individual remains the same, but different dreams are experienced. It also says that the magician does not change but creates illusions. Thus, Brahman does not change in spite of the changing world.

After establishing that Brahman is the source of everything by refuting other philosophies, the chapter goes on to establish that matter by itself cannot create something like clay and become a pot without a potter. So there is an Intelligence behind all creation. The Brahma Sutras state that there is an order in the universe. Where does that come from? So, atoms by themselves cannot be active without a law. Thus, philosophies that reduce the universe to atoms as the primary source of the physical Universe are refuted.

It goes onto refute other philosophies. One such philosophy states that the external and internal worlds are real. The internal world includes thoughts, emotions, impressions in the mind, dreams and so on. Another philosophy states that only ideas are real while yet another states that everything is void and unreal.* All of them, however, accept that everything is momentary or that nothing is permanent. These philosophies predate Buddhism and later commentators use these Sutras to refute Buddhist tenets. However, in the Brahma Sutras, there is no explicit reference to Buddhism; they refute only the earlier nascent forms that were in existence when the Brahma Sutras were composed. The essence of the argument in the Brahma Sutras is that if everything is momentary, what causes the atoms and other things to follow a cause or a pattern? If there is a cause, then that cause cannot be momentary. If there is no cause, it logically implies that matter—that is, everything in the internal and external world—should not be governed by a set of laws. That is, however, not the case. Memory is more permanent than thoughts and mental impressions. How, then, does memory arise if everything is momentary? Perhaps the Vedantic School says that the Law itself originates from Brahman and is the same as reality, Buddhism also talks of

---

* 'Shunya' or 'void' is a part of Buddhist philosophy and doctrine which came after the Brahma Sutras were written.

a Law but does not give it the status of reality.[*] This point can be summarized by the following phrase:

नासतः, दृष्टत्वात् ॥

Nāsataḥ, dṛṣṭatvāt

Na—Not; *asataḥ*—from non-existence; *dṛṣṭatvāt*—because this is not seen. Thus, this phrase can be translated as 'Existence does not result from non-existence, because this is not seen.'

Another philosophy states that we cannot say whether a thing is real or unreal—it can be both or neither and is essentially indescribable. This later evolved into the Jain philosophy. However, according to the Brahma Sutras, this is an impossible premise. Either the Soul changes, which is not possible, or it does not, which is inconsistent with the idea that it is not real (that which changes is not real). Later commentators quote from the Jain scriptures to refute the arguments, but there is no mention of Jainism in the Brahma Sutras. Like Buddhism, this type of philosophy predates Jainism but closely resembles it.[†]

---

[*] Here, the attempt is to state what the Brahma Sutras say and not to establish that they alone are 'right' or 'correct'.

[†] The interesting point is that various later philosophies in Buddhism and Jainism perhaps existed in a nascent form even earlier.

It also refutes other (Hindu) philosophies which believe in a God from whom the individual soul originates. The argument is that the individual soul cannot be created since creation also implies destruction whereas the soul cannot be destroyed by virtue of being immortal.

The difficulty in unravelling the Brahma Sutras becomes clear from the preceding discussion. The sutras are terse. Commentators then explain this using the Upanishads, selecting verses that adhere to their line of interpretation. This is one reason why the five major commentaries or *bhashyas* differ from each other. However, a few things are common among all the later interpretations that accept the primacy of the Upanishads and the Vedas. One point of commonality is the acceptance of Brahman as the origin and source of everything. Brahman is the efficient cause. The refutations of other philosophies ultimately try to establish this.

The third chapter is called *Sadhana Adhyaya* or the Study of *Sadhana*. 'Sadhana' refers to the methods for attaining the objective of life—knowledge of Brahman. The chapter is divided into four sections. The first section discusses the passage of the soul after death. It is said that there is no eternal heaven or hell. Good deeds take the soul to heaven, also known as *Chandraloka* or the realm of the moon. When the *karmas* or fruits of the good deeds are exhausted, the soul is reborn. Similarly, those who perform bad *karmas* go to hell or *Yamaloka*, and once they exhaust the fruits of their *karma*, they are reborn. Only those who have gained knowledge of Brahman during their lifetime or at the point of death escape rebirth. Good deeds include the performance of sacrifices as well as charitable work. No *karma* is added while in heaven or hell. The *jiva* is reborn and brings with it the residual *karmas* that have not been exhausted either in heaven or in hell. Heaven and hell are both temporary, and after exhausting part of one's *karma*, the soul is reborn. Human birth gives the *jiva* an opportunity to work out the *karmas* and obtain liberation or *moksha*. Scholars say that the purpose of this section is to create dispassion for the endless cycle of birth and death, suffering or enjoying the fruits of action. The language is also symbolic, using terms such as *Chandraloka* and *Yamaloka*.

In the next section of Chapter 3, the nature of the individual or *jiva* and the nature of Brahman are established by referring to the Upanishads. It says that the individual who goes through the states of waking, dreaming and deep sleep remains the same. Similarly, on swooning and recovering, they remain the same individual. This establishes that within the individual, there exists something which does not change. The nature of Brahman is also discussed and it is reiterated that there can be no two entities, that Brahman is only One. It is formless and can be experienced by the individual soul in the state of perfect meditation. This section also establishes that Ishwara or God is the giver of the fruits of action or *karma*.

The third section of the chapter first establishes that the *upasanas* or the methods of worship or invocation of Brahman are essentially the same in all the Upanishads. It reiterates that '*Om*', the sacred *mantra*, is a means of meditation. Knowledge, omniscience and bliss is to be meditated on as this is the very essence of Brahman and the Atman. Methods include meditating on the Atman as the origin of the universe, as the sky, as something all-pervading, as the mind, or as a light or a steady fire or flame. Such meditations are not to be combined but performed separately (based perhaps on individual temperament or instructions by a teacher). An individual who succeeds in such meditation has nothing further to obtain at the time of death since he has achieved liberation.

The fourth section of the chapter establishes that knowledge of Brahman is the purpose of life. It refutes counter-arguments which claim that the actions prescribed in the Karma Kanda of the Vedas are the goal of the Vedas rather than the Atman. The Brahma Sutras say that the *jiva* or individual is the agent referred to when Vedic rituals are performed, not the Atman which is distinct from the *jiva*. It refutes the argument that the Vedas only ask us to perform work rather than acquire knowledge. But work as a means to gain knowledge is accepted. It says that even those who do not want to gain *moksha* or liberation should follow the injunctions of the Vedas. Work is a means to obtaining the ultimate knowledge of the Atman. An example of such work is the work of controlling the senses and the mind. It also says that anyone is entitled to gain this knowledge irrespective of gender or marital status. This knowledge can be gained only in this life and not after death. The state of one who has gained that knowledge is the same and does not vary from one person to another.

The fourth and final chapter starts with exhortations to follow the *vidyas* or methods of gaining the knowledge of Brahman and then goes on to describe the result of that knowledge. It says that knowledge once gained, must be taught to others. It says that the seeker should not identify himself with the objects of meditation (the symbol 'Om', the mind, *prana* or breath and light or flame). The object of meditation, for instance Om, has to be thought of as Brahman, but Brahman is not to be thought of Om. That makes the meditation better. The benefits of knowing Brahman are described as bliss and the removal of the effects of *karma*. There is a discussion which says that those *karmas* that have not yet borne fruit are removed whereas those that have started bearing fruit are retained in experience, even though this does not in any way affect the liberated one. Later interpretations, however, have concluded that the *karmas* that have not yet started bearing fruit—known as *sanchita karma*—are destroyed. The *agami karma*—*karmas* which arise out of current work—do not arise for the liberated individual as they no longer perform work with a sense of agency. The *prarabdha karma*—*karmas* that have started bearing fruit—are apparently experienced and, upon their exhaustion, the individual achieves *videha mukti* which is liberation after death.

In the second section of the chapter, a distinction is made about the actual mode of liberation between the knowers of *nirguna* Brahman (Brahman without attributes) and the *saguna* Brahman (Brahman with attributes). The sense organs are merged in the mind which is then merged with the *prana* or life energy. This is also true of ordinary *jivas* irrespective of whether they have realized Brahman. For the ordinary *jivas*, the *prana* departs and there is rebirth. For the knowers of *saguna* Brahman, the *prana* goes to *Brahmaloka* and from there it gets liberated. For the knowers of *nirguna* Brahman, the *prana* does not depart from the body but merges with Brahman.*

---

* This may not apply fully but two incidents can be cited to illustrate the merging of the *prana* with Brahman in knowers of *nirguna* Brahman. Palani Swami, a companion of Ramana Maharshi, a 20th-century sage, was served by the Maharshi in his dying moments. The Maharshi said that when he passed away, Palani Swami opened his eyes and his soul escaped, indicating he may have obtained liberation through the path of *Brahmaloka*. The Maharshi was with his mother also until she passed away.

The third section is even more esoteric or mystical and describes the path taken by the knower of *saguna* Brahman after death. It describes the various stages the *jiva* or individual soul goes through and the paths of the *devas* or gods that it crosses before it finally merges with Brahman.

The final section of the last chapter talks about the end or goal attained by the liberated *jiva*. The knowers of *nirguna* Brahman simply merge with Brahman and there is nothing else after this. The knowers of *saguna* Brahman are manifest as pure, without sin. They can, by their mere will, realize all desires (which are not of this world). They can exist with or without a body, as in dreams. The desires are experienced as in dreams without a body. Such a liberated *jiva* in *Brahmaloka* has all the powers, except that of Ishwara, that is, the power of creating the universe. It closes with the final *sutra* which says that there is no return to this world for liberated souls.

Some Notes

There are other interpretations of the Brahma Sutras. Advaita says that Brahman is formless and attribute-less.

The Maharshi said that the *jiva* of his mother had merged within and that she had obtained liberation, a reference perhaps to *nirguna* liberation.

All other interpretations, including the Visishtadvaita and the Dvaita, agree that Brahman is the Supreme Reality and has attributes. They also say that Narayana or Vishnu, a Personal God is the same as Brahman. According to Visishtadvaita, Brahman is qualified by the universe and living beings, whereas Dvaita maintains that Brahman is separate from them. The two philosophies also differ about the concept of liberation. Visishtadvaita says liberation is freedom from rebirth, but the *jiva* or individual soul goes to Vaikuntha (which is similar to *Brahmaloka*) and enjoys eternal bliss in the company of Narayana. All souls are identical to each other and, in essence, the same as Brahman. Dvaita, however, says that the soul is merely a reflection of Brahman, eternally dependent on it and even in essence is different from it. Liberation is also freedom from rebirth. The quantum of bliss enjoyed depends on the worthiness of each liberated soul and is different for different souls. Unlike Advaita, the other philosophies do not accept *jivan mukti* or liberation while in the body. According to them, liberation can take place only after the body has perished.

Overview of the Six Philosophies

The following chart gives a brief overview of all the Six Darsanas:

Philosophy or *Darsana*	Nyaya or Tarka Sastra	Vaiseshika	Sankhya	Yoga	Purva Mimamsa	Vedanta or Uttara Mimamsa
Basis	Logical realism. Accepts what we perceive and experience as real	Physical world reduced to atoms. Admits non-material soul of man and God	Realism, dualism and pluralism, and knowledge	Control of the mind and senses	The earlier part of the Vedas, that is, the Samhita and the Brahmanas	Logic and the Upanishads
Knowledge and its tests	Four means of knowledge: perception, inference, comparison, testimony	Original texts say that perception and inference are the two bases of knowledge	Knowledge through perception, inference, testimony	No theory of knowledge per se; borrows from Sankhya	Vedic rituals are supreme. *Mimamsa* or logic is used to interpret and infer the rituals	Direct spiritual experience
Universe	God creates, protects, destroys and re-creates the universe	Universe categorized into substance, quality, activity, generality, particularity, inherent attributes and non-existence	One Nature, several Purushas or souls. Describes twenty-four principles of the universe, the three *gunas*	Accepts earlier views. Has no separate theory about the universe	Vedas are eternal, therefore God did not create them. Vedas are not produced by man (*apaurusheya*), but are eternal and infinite	Is a manifestation of the Supreme Reality; either pervaded by God or is separate from God
Man and his ultimate goal	Liberation	Liberation	Liberation	Liberation	Follow *dharma*, which are the Vedic rituals	Liberation

	'Proves' that God exists by using empirical evidence and logic	God creates the universe, but does not pervade it	Some texts accept God whereas others do not	Explicitly accepts God as an important means to liberation	Does not accept God as the creator or as the giver of the fruits of action	Accepts God
Views on God						
Texts	Gautama's Nyaya Sutra, approx. 400 BCE. Several commentaries up to 1650 CE	Kanada's Vaiseshika Sutra, 400 BCE. Several commentaries exist	Kapila's Sankhya Sutra, now lost. Sankhya Karika or commentary of Isvara Krishna as well as later texts	Patanjali's Yoga Sutras and later commentaries	Jaimini's Mimamsa Sutra and several commentaries and later texts	Badarayana's Brahma Sutras. Also called the Vedanta Sutras and the Bhikshu Sutras
Remarks	Uses logic. Accepts the authority of the Vedas but does not use it explicitly	Closely linked to the Nyaya. Cause and effect are different. For instance, cloth is new and different from its threads	Psychology of mind, intelligence, ego and modifications of the mind-stuff stored in memory	Yoga here refers to the union of the Self with God or Brahman		Brahma Sutras and the Upanishads are the basis of various Vedanta philosophies such as the Advaita, Visishtadvaita and Dvaita, Shuddhadvaita, Dvaita-Advaita and Achintya Bheda Abheda

Summary and Some Notes

The Brahma Sutras establish what the Upanishads say, discuss the goal of human life and provide some suggestions about how to reach that goal. It says that the goal of life is liberation.

Of the Six Darsanas, the Brahma Sutras are the only one that refer directly to the Upanishads. Three others—the Nyaya, Vaiseshika and Sankhya—do not refer to the Vedas or Upanishads but simply accept their supremacy. They use reason and logic to establish their doctrines. The Yoga Sutras do not even contain a philosophy per se. They are a practical treatise on how to reach the goal of union of the individual soul with the Divine. The Purva Mimamsa refers only to the earlier sections of the Vedas which emphasize rituals and ignores the Upanishads.

Of the Six Darsanas, only two—the Brahma Sutras and the Yoga Sutras—are studied today by serious seekers. The Brahma Sutras offer a philosophical basis for the revelations of the Upanishads while the Yoga Sutras provide a method of reaching the goal of life.

6

THE BHAGAVAD GITA

The Bhagavad Gita is perhaps the most widely known and respected scripture in Hinduism. It is part of the *prasthana traya*, the three most sacred scriptures that also include the Upanishads and the Brahma Sutras. Since there are references to the Vedas in the Gita and a few of its verses are quoted from the Upanishads almost verbatim, it may be inferred that the Gita was composed later. There are numerous translations and commentaries on this text from ancient times down to the present day. Translations are available in all Indian languages as well as in English, French, German, Dutch, Italian, Portuguese, Spanish, Chinese, Japanese, Arabic, Hebrew, Greek, Serbian and Russian.

The Gita has 700 Sanskrit verses and is a part of the Mahabharata which has over 100,000 verses. It is widely believed that it was Adi Sankara who brought the Gita into prominence with his commentary.

Since this text is the most translated, commented, and interpreted of the scriptures, we will discuss only those ideas which appear for the first time in the Gita as a fully developed teaching or philosophy. One major departure is that the teaching is through a Personal God in human form called an *avatar* or incarnation of God. The word '*avatar*' means 'descent', implying the descent of God in human form. This idea is also present in the Puranas which say that there are ten main incarnations of God. However, the earlier *avatars* do not come forth as teachers who explicitly teach. The Upanishads are poetic outpourings of the *rishis* about the revelations and truths realized by them. The names of many of the *rishis* remain unknown. The idea of God in human form is absent in the Upanishads. Thus, what we have in the Gita is the first appearance of a God (in the form of Krishna) who is bold enough to teach.* He also refers to himself as an incarnation of God. The idea of God and His worship as a means to salvation is a central aspect of the teaching.

We also see different teachings suitable for people with different temperaments. The earlier Upanishads do not have a well-developed philosophy and teaching. The Gita, by contrast, expounds the philosophies of Karma Yoga (the Yoga of selfless work), Bhakti Yoga (the Yoga of devotion), *Dhyana Yoga* (the Yoga of meditation) and Jnana Yoga

---

* Rama, an earlier *avatar*, does give teaching in the Adhyatma Ramayana, a text which includes the Rama Gita. However, this text was written several centuries later.

(the Yoga of knowledge). There are explicit teachings for the sincere seeker that are intended to help them live a better and more fulfilling life. The Gita also has chapters on God and the world, a discussion on *upasana* or worship of the Manifest and Unmanifest God, philosophical teachings about the knower, the known and knowledge and discussions about what happens to the individual on his way to salvation as well as the characteristics of the illumined or emancipated soul.

In contrast to the Upanishads which appeal perhaps only to those attracted by a purely spiritual quest for the Truth, the Gita is set in the battlefield and addresses Arjuna who, in fact, is not even seeking the Truth. Arjuna admits that he is confused and finds it difficult to control the mind and wishes to know what happens to someone who, despite following the teachings fails to reach the goal. These are questions which probably occur to many people, a feature which makes the Gita universally accessible. The Gita is thus addressed to everyone.

A new, fully developed idea appears for the first time. This is the Yoga of selfless work or Karma Yoga. It is based on a clear understanding of the individual and the human condition. The first premise is that man is bound to act and cannot sit idle. Even thinking, dreaming, breathing and so on are regarded as actions. These actions create impressions in the mind which in turn, become the cause of further action, since it is human nature to repeat actions that provide joy or pleasure and avoid those that bring pain and suffering. Over time, these impressions strengthen, leading to desire and aversion and become the cause for further action. This leads to an endless chain of cause and effect which binds us. Krishna offers a way forward for those bound by this karmic law of cause and effect. The Gita says that by performing work without attachment to its results, we free ourselves from the impressions created in the mind. The most famous verse embodying this teaching is

कर्मण्येवाधिकारस्ते मा फलेषु कदाचन |
मा कर्मफलहेतुर्भूर्मा ते सङ्गोऽस्त्वकर्मणि || 2.47 ||

Karmaṇyevādhikāraste mā phaleṣu kadācana
Mā karmaphalaheturbhūrmā te saṅgo'stvakarmaṇi

[You have the right to work alone and not to the fruits (of work). Do not be impelled by the fruits of work, nor be attached to inaction.]

Several commentaries have been written on this verse. Why does the Gita say this? For the faithful, the teaching itself is enough and they try to follow this dictum. For others, however, reason is required. Even for those who have faith, some questions remain. What is the meaning of the fruits of work? Should we not worry about the results of work? If results are immaterial, how can we do the work effectively?

This teaching is perhaps for all people who are caught in a dilemma about the right course of action. Arjuna is in the middle of the battlefield and wonders whether it is right to fight one's relatives and friends or whether it is better to withdraw. Krishna exhorts him to fight but without attachment to the fruits of work. The 'fruit' most probably refers to the karmic fruit, that is, the acceptance of the inner psychological results of action—elation on victory and dejection on defeat. Once you detach yourself from this, you free yourself internally from the consequences of the action. No fresh binding impressions are created in the mind for further action. In another sense, since the results of action are inevitable and decided by the laws of cause and effect, the individual should not worry about them. There is a strongly held theory that the giver of the fruits of action is Ishwara or the Lord Himself. So, one has no right over it. However, even if one does not believe in an Ishwara, there is an inevitable consequence of action. Does that mean that one refrains from action altogether? Krishna says again, no, do not be attached to inaction. Action is inevitable as no one can sit idle. The only way to become free is to detach oneself from the fruits of action. Implicit in this is the fact that we are all subject to the impressions in our own minds and experience happiness or sorrow due to them. One of the ways of freeing oneself from such emotion is shown by this verse. The mind which is attached to pleasure cannot also be detached from suffering. If we are attached to the fruits of action, we must also accept the impressions in our minds, both good and bad. Performing detached action consciously is one way of becoming free. The teaching is a means of eventually gaining freedom from one's own *karmas*—from the endless chain of cause and effect.

The idea of selfless work is present even in the Vedas, although there it refers to the Vedic *karmas* or rituals. If these *karmas* are performed with detachment, the mind is purified. A similar idea is found in the Upanishads as well. The king, Janaka learns from his teacher, Yajnavalkya in the Brihadaranyaka Upanishad and is initiated into the path of Truth, following which he continues to perform his royal duties in a detached manner. However, in the Gita, this idea is fully developed.

Another departure from the Upanishads is the idea of devotion to a Personal God as a means to liberation. The Upanishads are almost entirely about realization of Brahman which is not a Personal God. Even though the idea of Ishwara is present in the Upanishads, it is more of an abstract concept. Ishwara refers to that aspect of Brahman which is manifest and rules the universe. It is difficult to develop any devotion to such an abstract entity. However, in the Gita, Krishna says that those who show devotion to a Personal God can also gain salvation. Devotion to God has perhaps the widest appeal as compared to other paths. One of the most oft-quoted verses on this subject is:

सर्वधर्मान्परित्यज्य मामेकं शरणं व्रज |
अहं त्वा सर्वपापेभ्यो मोक्षयिष्यामि मा शुचः || 18.66 ||

Sarva dharman parityajya mamekam saranam vraja
Aham tva sarvapapebhyo moksha ishyami ma suchah

[Renouncing all *dharmas*, take refuge in Me alone. I will free you from all sin, I promise.*]

The Gita contains other teachings on devotion. This verse comes at the end of the Gita when all other *yogas* have been expounded. Several commentaries have also been written on this one verse. The idea of surrender to God alone is emphasized here. Without giving up attachment to other things, such surrender is not possible since the mind will invariably wander to those things. Krishna promises that he will give salvation to those who genuinely surrender. This verse comes after a series of verses exhorting Arjuna to follow the teachings. It says a few verses earlier 'Isvarah sarvabhutanam', the Lord dwells in all beings. In the next

---

* Similar statements are made by Jesus Christ: 'I am the way and the truth and the life. No one comes to the Father except through me. If you really know me, you will know my Father as well' (John 4:16).

set of verses, Krishna asks Arjuna to fix his mind on God, to be devoted to God, bow down to God and so on, using the word 'Me' to refer to God. This is followed by the famous verse quoted here. Since the Lord dwells in all beings, commentators have said that it is not to a person that we surrender but to the spirit that dwells within, be that within Krishna or our Atman. Krishna refers to that Self or Atman within him and within all beings rather than to his human personality when he uses the word 'Me'. The word 'alone' implies that all other distractions are gone and the mind is focused fully on the Atman. Commentators have interpreted this as the surrender of the ego. Dissolving the ego in the Atman is considered final liberation.* Other commentators place emphasis on Krishna as the *avatar* who alone can deliver the human soul when it is surrendered to him. Each reader will interpret these verses in their own way, something which is probably for the best as long as it is done with sincerity.

Krishna explicitly declares himself as an *avatar*, which seems to have no other scriptural precedent. Although Rama is also regarded as an *avatar*, we do not come across such a clear statement from him.

---

* Buddhism says *anatta*—removal of the ego—is *nirvana*. Christianity also refers to the surrender of the ego, and the word '*Islam*' itself means surrender or submission to the will to God.

अजोऽपि सन्नव्ययात्मा भूतानामीश्वरोऽपि सन् |
प्रकृतिं स्वामधिष्ठाय संभवाम्यात्ममायया || 4.6||

*ajo 'pi sannavyayātmā bhūtānām īshvaro 'pi san
prakritim svām adhishṭhāya sambhavāmyātma-māyayā*

[Though I am unborn and my Self is imperishable,
though I am the Lord of all creatures, I come into being
through the power of my *maya*.]

This coming into being refers to physical birth and
'*maya*' refers to the power through which the universe is
created. The following two verses (both of which are very
well-known) also state this explicitly. In them, Krishna
says that whenever there is a decline of *dharma* (or
righteousness) and the rise of unrighteousness, He will be
incarnated: 'O Bharata (O Arjuna), I incarnate Myself.
For the protection of the good and the destruction of the
wicked and the establishment of righteousness, I come
forth from age to age.'

In the *Jnana Yoga* of the Gita, there are a series of verses
aimed at striving towards knowledge. Starting with action,
the Gita says that one should give up selfish desire in action

---

* Christ observes, 'The Father and I are one', thereby declaring his
identity with God.

यस्य सर्वे समारम्भाः कामसङ्कल्पवर्जिताः

yasya sarve samārambhāḥ kāma-saṅkalpa-varjitāḥ

[(He who) gives up selfish desire in action]

त्यक्त्वा कर्मफलासङ्गं

Tyaktva karmaphala sanga

[Gives up the fruits of action]

निराशीर्यतचित्तात्मा

Nirasir yata chittatma

[Free from desires and with mind under control]

It goes onto say that the senses and vital forces should be brought under control. Some offer their material possessions, some offer their *tapas* or striving and yet others offer their learning and knowledge. This indicates that the effort is offered as a sacrifice with the aim of reaching the goal of spiritual life. It refers to *pranayama* (loosely translated as 'breath control') and regulation of food intake. But among all these sacrifices, it goes onto say that striving for knowledge is superior to any other material striving, since all actions ultimately lead to knowledge. Arjuna is asked to go and learn that knowledge in a spirit of humility from those who have realized the Truth. The ones who have attained this knowledge are described as 'wise'. They never fall into confusion again and are able to see all existence in the Self. All (past) sins are overcome and just as fire burns everything to ashes, all impressions created by action are destroyed. One oft-quoted verse is:

श्रद्धावाँल्लभते ज्ञानं तत्परः संयतेन्द्रियः |
ज्ञानं लब्ध्वा परां शान्तिमचिरेणाधिगच्छति ||

Shraddhavan labhate jnanam, tatparah samyat indriyah
Jnanam labdhva param santim achirane adhigacchyat.
(4.39)

[Those with faith gain knowledge, and he who has subdued his senses gains knowledge that brings supreme peace.]

In the *Dhyana Yoga*, the state of mind of the *yogi* is described as steady as the flame of a lamp in a windless place. '*Yoga*' refers to the state of mind at rest and is achieved by concentration. This gives supreme joy. Once established in that state, the *yogi* does not fall away from it. There is nothing to be gained beyond this and the *yogi* is not shaken even by great sorrow. All selfish desires have to be abandoned and the mind made tranquil gradually through concentration. This gives supreme bliss. This state is also described in the following verse:

यो मां पश्यति सर्वत्र सर्वं च मयि पश्यति

Yo maam pasyati sarvatra, sarvancha mayi pasyati

[One who sees Me everywhere and sees all in Me]

Here, 'Me' refers to the Self or Atman. Arjuna asks, perhaps on behalf of all people, how the mind which is so restless can be made tranquil. The answer acknowledges that the mind is indeed difficult to control and provides the method in yet another oft-quoted phrase:

अभ्यासेन तु कौन्तेय वैराग्येण च गृह्यते

Abhyasena tu Kaunteya vairagyena cha grihyate

[Through constant practice and detachment, O Arjuna, it can be done.]

There are often words of reassurance. Arjuna asks what happens to those who strive but do not reach the goal. Krishna says there is no destruction for such persons, and they get the chance to reach the goal through a favourable environment in their next birth.

All the different paths have some common bases. Arjuna is asked to be detached, keep the mind calm, have equanimity, faith, not be egotistical and follow the middle path between austerity and indulgence. This state of mind must be cultivated irrespective of the path followed.

The Gita is in harmony with the Vedas and Upanishads. It refers to them and accepts their authority. It also refers to the twin symbols of '*Om*' and 'Light:

ओमित्येकाक्षरं ब्रह्म

Om ityeksharam Brahma

[Om alone is that imperishable Brahman (as said in several Upanishads).]

It goes on to say that one should meditate on Om as it leads to the highest goal. Referring to the Atman and Brahman, it says:

ज्योतिषामपि तज्ज्योतिस्तमसः परमुच्यते

jyotishām api taj jyotis tamasaḥ parama uchyate

[The Light of lights beyond all darkness]

The Gita clearly states that the Truth can be known by *pratyaksha avagamam* or direct experience. It also compares different types of aspirants and says that those who seek the Unmanifest face much greater difficulty because it is hard to reach for embodied beings. But those who seek a manifest Personal God have an easier path. Therefore, as far as possible, the mind should be fixed on that Personal God. In case that fails, the individual should focus their mind through steady concentration. If neither is possible, the individual should either perform all actions for that God or surrender to that God. Thus, different forms of worship are given for different types of devotees or aspirants.

Summary and Conclusions

Since a vast body of literature is widely available on the Gita, this chapter has been kept short. The teachings of the Gita have a much wider appeal because, unlike the Upanishads which are addressed to those who have retired to the forest, they are addressed to people living in the world. It has all three aspects: revelation, metaphysics or philosophy that explains the revelations and practical teachings about what to do in one's day-to-day life. It does not prescribe rituals, but tells you what to do and, equally important, what attitude and frame of mind to adopt. It does not merely prescribe but also provides the reasons for these practical teachings. God is explicitly mentioned and is a central part of its teaching. Together with the content, it is perhaps these universal aspects which account for the wide appeal and enduring popularity of the Bhagavad Gita.

It is said that:

सर्वोपनिषदो गावो, दोग्धा गोपाल नन्दन: |
पार्थो वत्स: सुधीर्भोक्ता, दुग्धं गीतामृतं महत् ||

Sarvopanishado gaavo, dogdhaa gopala nandana:
paarthovatsa: sudheerbhoktaa, dugdham gitaamrutam
mahat

[If all the Upanishads are cows, Gopala Nandana (Krishna) is the milker and Arjuna is the calf, then the milk of the Gita is the nectar (of immortality) that is drunk by the wise.]

In simpler terms, this couplet says that the Gita is the very essence of the Upanishads, is as easy to drink as milk and confers immortality.

7

PURANAS

The word *'purana'* literally means 'old'. Although there are references to the Puranas in the Vedas, some are considered to have been composed as late as the medieval period. Thus, these texts span millennia. However, most of the Puranas are ancient and were composed after the Vedas. The Puranas and the two epics, Ramayana and Mahabharata are part of popular Hinduism. There are eighteen major Puranas or Mahapuranas, namely Brahma, Padma, Vishnu, Siva, Bhagavata, Narada, Markandeya, Agni, Bhavishya, Brahmavaivarta, Linga, Varaha, Skanda, Vamana, Kurma, Matsya, Garuda and Brahmanda. In addition, there are eighteen minor or Upapuranas. It is estimated that together they have over 400,000 verses in Sanskrit. By contrast, the Bhagavad Gita has only 700 verses.

The Puranas discuss cosmology and have stories about the creation of the universe, gods, sages, kings, heroes as well as ordinary people. There are stories with a moral and ethical meaning as well as philosophy. They are intended to convey the essence of religion in a simple way.

According to Puranic lore, Brahma is said to be the Creator of the Universe, Vishnu the Sustainer or Preserver and Siva the One who finally dissolves the Universe. According to the Puranas, the world as we see it will dissolve, and later there will be yet another creation. This cycle of creation and dissolution of the universe continues forever. Brahma, Vishnu and Siva emerged from Brahman, the transcendental, formless, eternal Truth mentioned in the Upanishads. However, there are many versions of this in different Puranas.

The Vaishnava Puranas about Vishnu and His Incarnations are well-known across India. In Puranic lore, Siva appears as Dakshinamurthi as well as a teacher to great sages, although he does not take birth in human form. Some of the Puranas are about Brahma, the Creator who has no human incarnation. In addition to these three gods, there are references to many other gods and goddesses in the Puranas.

The concept of the descent of God's incarnation on earth as an *avatar* in the form of a human being is developed in the Puranas. The well-known idea of the '*Dasavataras*' or ten *avatars* is found in several Puranas, although there are slight variations among them. According to one text, this list includes Matsya (fish), Kurma (tortoise), Varaha (boar), Narasimha (half-man, half-lion), Vamana, Parasurama,

Rama, Krishna, Buddha and the yet-to-come Kalki. In some texts, Buddha is substituted by Balarama whereas in some others, Parasurama is replaced by Balarama. However, the Bhagavata Purana is clear about one fact— that Krishna is not an *avatar* but God Himself and the source from whom all other *avatars* emerged. It goes on to list twenty-four *avatars*, many of whom are regarded as partial manifestations. Some of them include Veda Vyasa, Kapila, Nara-Narayana (the twin manifestation of God and His close human friend) who exist for the welfare of the world and Dattatreya who combines the attributes of Brahma, Vishnu and Siva.

It is Vishnu who takes human birth as an *avatar* while Brahma and Siva do not.* Siva, however, manifests himself occasionally through special human beings. The sage, Sankaracharya is considered to be one such special individual. Dakshinamurthi, though not human, manifests as Siva to chosen spiritual aspirants and devotees. The central idea seems to be that God is accessible and manifests Himself from time to time to redeem devotees.

Some popular and powerful figures emerge in the Puranas. For instance, the four 'mind-born' sons of the creator Brahma.† They disobeyed Brahma by remaining

---

* Vishnu is the Immanent God that resides in the universe. Siva is transcendent and cannot be easily manifested.
† They are Sanaka, Sanatana, Sanandana and Sanatkumara.

celibate though they were created to populate the earth. They are said to be eternally free souls who are always young, and go about the earth, heavens, *Brahmaloka* and other worlds teaching. Brahma then created ten other mind-born sons such as Atri, Bhrigu, Narada, Vasishtha and so on. Of the first four children, Sanatkumara taught Narada the highest Truths in the Chandogya Upanishad. Narada is well-known all over India as a sage who preaches devotion to God.

One popular story is about Narada who thinks he is the best among all devotees of Lord Vishnu. Vishnu, however, says that one ordinary farmer is more devoted to Him. Narada is surprised to hear this and visits the farmer. He worked hard the whole day, carried out his family duties and prays to God only very briefly. Narada is puzzled and tells Vishnu that he remembers Him day and night, while the farmer hardly prays to God. Vishnu then asks him to take a pot filled to the brim with oil and go around the field without spilling a drop. When Narada accomplishes this feat, Vishnu asks him, 'How many times did you remember me?' 'O! Lord! How could I think of you? My mind was concentrated on the oil!' Then Vishnu says, 'See how great the farmer is. In spite of so many duties, he remembers me every day.' The moral of the story is interpreted in various way. Devotion is not measured by external rituals, dress and markings, nor by the amount of time spent in prayer, but by performing one's duty and selflessly offering the results to God. Even an ordinary individual can be a great devotee. The thought that I am a great devotee fattens the ego and needs to be removed. Vishnu in fact teaches this lesson to Narada through the farmer.

The story of *Samudra Manthan* (literally, 'churning the ocean') is well-known across India. This story with slight variations is there in the Bhagavat and Vishnu Puranas as well as in the Mahabharata. The *devas* (gods) and *asuras* (demons) had a great battle in which the gods were vanquished and the demons emerged victorious. The gods went to Lord Vishnu and implored him to save them. Vishnu said only Amrutam, the nectar of immortality, could save them. However, this could only be obtained from the *Ksheera Sagara,* the Ocean of Milk. The ocean would need to be churned to extract Amrutam. The *asuras* were co-opted to churn the ocean since the task required huge effort. The mountain, Mandara,* served as the anchor

---

* 'The Mandara mountains were formed millions of years ago when a continental plate of basement rock deep beneath the African continent rose up, fragmenting and splitting as it was pushed to the surface. The climate was significantly wetter in those times, so enormous amounts of precipitation formed numerous rivers that rushed through these fractures, carving them deeper and wider, resulting in the range's notably rugged terrain.

Volcanic activity also played a role in the formation of the range. Eruptions of lava formed volcanic cones whose vents were eventually plugged with hardening magma. These hardened cores are called volcanic plugs. In the case of the Mandara Mountains, the plugs were much more erosion-resistant than the exterior of the cones, which

or churning rod and was put into the ocean by Vishnu. A gigantic rope was required which would be pulled from two ends of the ocean. This would rotate the mountain, churn the ocean and eventually bring out the nectar from its depths. The analogy of churning milk in this way to extract butter is well- known in India as this is the technique that was followed in households until recently. The giant snake Vasuki coiled around Lord Siva's neck, was used as the rope. The *asuras* held the head of the snake and the *devas* the tail. They churned the ocean for a thousand years. The mountain started sinking. Lord Vishnu took the form of a tortoise, Kurma and went under the ocean to hold up the earth. This is regarded as the second *avatar* or Incarnation of Vishnu. The poison *halahal* emanating from the mouth of the great snake Vasuki was so dangerous it would have destroyed the world. It was swallowed by Lord Siva and this saved the world. He is called *Nilakantha*, the Blue-Throated One, as the poison turned his throat blue. In one version of this story, the Divine Mother Parvati, wife of Siva, pressed his throat so that the poison did not enter his stomach and was retained in his throat. Thus Lord Siva came be known as the one who swallows the poison of the world to save humankind.

---

wore away over time. Eventually, only the plugs remained, forming the stark, needle-like spires such as Kapsiki Peak that the range is known for.' See Wikipedia, accessed 14 May 2022, source: https://en.wikipedia.org/wiki/Mandara_Mountains.

In the process of this churning, several precious things emerged. The wish-fulfilling sacred cow, Kamadhenu emerged and was given to the sages. The seven-headed horse, Uchhaishravas was given to the *asuras* and Airavata, the celestial white elephant was taken by Indra, the King of the *devas*. These *devas* were always subservient to the Supreme Gods, Vishnu and Siva. Parijat, the tree with never fading scented blossoms was taken to *swarga* or heaven. The *asuras* took Varuni, the creator of intoxicants like wine. Lakshmi the Goddess of Wealth emerged and married Vishnu. The moon or Chandra emerged and adorned Lord Siva's hair. This is why Siva is also known as Chandrasekhara. Dhanavantri, the divine doctor emerged with the pot of nectar, Amrutam, and also became a physician to heal humankind. Lord Vishnu's *vahana* or vehicle, the great eagle Garuda emerged. Prayag, Ujjain, Haridwar and Nasik received a few drops of the nectar and became sacred sites. The Immortal nectar Amrutam was taken away by Garuda was first distributed to the *devas* by Lord Vishnu's. By the time the turn of the *asuras* came, the nectar was finished. Meanwhile one *asura* disguised himself and joined the *devas* and took Amrutam. When he was discovered, his head was cut off and split into two. Rahu swallows the sun during the solar eclipse and Ketu swallows the moon during a lunar eclipse. They are nevertheless immortal and are well-known figures in astrology. When the *asuras* realized that they were being cheated, they wanted to fight and claim their share. However, they were bewitched by Mohini, a celestial damsel and lost the opportunity to take *Amrutam*. Mohini, in fact, was Lord Vishnu himself in disguise. A few other precious things emerged from the *manthan* and different versions are recorded in different Puranic texts. Thus the *devas* regained their strength with Amrutam and defeated the *asuras*.

Various interpretations have been given for this story. The common points of various interpretations are the emergence of wealth, prosperity, health (which went to the *devas*) and intoxicants (which went to the *asuras*). The *devas* are benign gods who became immortal whereas the *asuras* are evil forces who were defeated. The *devas* represent the good qualities within us while the *asuras* represent the evil qualities. Amrutam makes us immortal and destroys the evil in us. Myths of creation as well as the primordial victory of good over evil are intertwined in this story.

Some Puranic texts extol sacred locations. The Skanda Purana says that the sacred hill Arunachala is where Siva resides. Similar references are there about Varanasi or Kashi. In the Vaishnava Puranas, Mathura and Vrindavan are extolled as sacred. Famous temples exist in these places even today and continue to attract large crowds of devotees.

There are stories about the origin of the Universe in various Puranas. They refer to the different *lokas* or worlds. The highest are Satyaloka (or *Brahmaloka*), where Truth prevails and *Tapaloka*, the world of austerity. The earth or *Bhuloka* is much lower, and below the earth exist further worlds which finally end in *Patalaloka* or the nether world. Some texts describe the origin of the universe and the birth of the sun, the moon and the earth. There are references to all the planets revolving around the sun on one plane, an observation which is in keeping with the discoveries of modern astronomy. Some of the stories can be interpreted in a manner consistent with the discoveries of modern science.[1]

A few well-known stories that influence popular religion even today are from the Puranas. Siva is an ascetic, who smears His body with ashes. His wife Sati is the daughter of Daksha the King of Mountains. She married Siva against her father's wishes. Daksha insults Siva in a public function. Sati dies of humiliation. Sati's death causes Siva to enter into a divine frenzy and carries the dead body and all over the world. Cosmic harmony is disturbed. The *devas* pray to Vishnu who intervenes by cutting off various parts of Sati's body. These parts are then scattered and the sites on which they fall come to be known as '*Sakti peethas*', which can be translated as 'centres of the Divine Mother's energy'. There are said to be eighteen such locations where the body parts had fallen. Even today, hundreds of thousands of pilgrims flock to these temples. Some of the well-known ones are Kamakshi in Kanchi, Chamundeswari in Mysuru, Bramarambha in

Srisailam, Kamakhya in Assam, Visalakshi in Varanasi and Srinkhala in West Bengal.

Another Puranic story which continues to be influential in the present day is that of the *Jyotirlingas*, literally 'emblems of light'. According to the Skanda Purana, Brahma and Vishnu tried to establish their supremacy. They had to find the top and bottom of a cosmic pillar of light which extended above and below. Neither could find the end of this pillar of light. The story suggests that Siva is great. Wherever Siva appeared as a column of Light, He was worshipped. According to a well-known Sanskrit verse, there are twelve such locations, with the most famous site located in Varanasi. The locations are Somnath, Srisailam, Ujjain, Omkareshwar, Vaidyanath, Bhimashankar, Rameswaram, Nagaeswara in Dwarka, Viswesvar in Varanasi, Nasik, Kedarnath in the Himalayas and Grishneshwar in Maharashtra. However, there are sometimes more than one location with the same name as in the case of Vaidyanath. Devotees flock to these temples in large numbers especially on days sacred to Siva including Mondays and Sivaratri, as well as the full moon.

Perhaps the Bhagavata Purana is the most widely read. It begins with an interesting story. King Parikshit is cursed to die of a snake bite in seven days. The divine sage, Suka arrives and narrates the Bhagavata Purana to him since it is the most liberating scripture. It has several interesting stories. One of the stories is about Ajamila, a great sinner. At the time of death, he calls out to his son, Narayana which is also one of the names of God. Ajamila is redeemed. The moral of the story is that if we remember God at the time of our death, we are saved no matter how many sins we might have committed. The story of the devotee Prahlada is well known. His father, Hiranyakashyapa was an *asura* who did not believe in God. But Prahlada was unshakeable in his devotion. Enraged by his son's devotion, Hiranyakashyapa tried to kill his son several times but failed. At last Vishnu himself appears as Narasimha—the Man-Lion—and kills Hiranyakashyapa. The king had obtained a boon that he could not be killed during the day or at night, inside or outside the house, by man, woman or beast. So he is killed at the doorstep at twilight by a Man Lion. '*Narasimha*' or '*Narsing*' is a common name and there are several temples to this *avatar* of Vishnu in south India. Prahlada exhibits several virtues and is extolled as the greatest of devotees. He forgives his father, never shows any anger and is always full of humility. The story of Gajendra Moksham is also well-known. The elephant, Gajendra (literally, 'king of elephants') is caught by a crocodile. After various attempts to free itself, it finally appeals to God and Vishnu saves him from the crocodile. The story of Ahalya (which also appears in the Ramayana) narrates how Ahalya, who had been cursed to become a stone, was also redeemed by Vishnu in the form of Lord Rama.

The Bhagavata Purana is full of stories about Lord Krishna. As a baby, his mother Yashoda looked into his mouth and saw the entire universe, including the sun, moon and the stars. The baby Krishna also suckled at the breasts of the demoness, Putana who was sent by Kamsa, the evil king, to kill him. However, instead of Krishna, it is Putana who dies and is, in fact, liberated. There is another story about the killing of the giant snake, Kaliya whose poison threatened the safety of all people. At the time of death, Kaliya says 'O Lord! You gave me poison and I worshipped you with it.' The stories of the young Krishna playing the flute and enchanting both his friends and the young girls (called *gopis*) have inspired numerous songs that are sung even today. Yet another story narrates how the child Krishna lifted the hill named Govardhan on his little finger in order to save the people from a deluge.

The descent of the Ganges from heaven is a tale recounted in many texts, including the Bhagavata Purana. Bhagiratha prays for thousands of years and brings the Ganges down from heaven so that its waters would purify the ashes of his ancestors and liberate them. However, the force of the waters makes everyone fear that the earth itself would be destroyed. Lord Siva takes the waters on his head, following which they flow through his locks and descend more gently upon the earth. On the way, the waters destroy the hermitage of sage Jahnu who drinks up the Ganges in anger. On being supplicated by Bhagiratha, the waters are again released from his ear. Another name of the Ganges is thus Jahnavi, the daughter of sage Jahnu.

Another famous prayer in the Bhagavata Purana is from one Rantideva. He was a King who gave up everything. He offered prayers to God to free his people from the miseries inflicted by a terrible famine. After forty-eight days of fasting, he reluctantly agreed to eat when his former ministers brought food. At that very moment, however, he was visited by people who were starving. Moved by their plight, Rantideva gave away everything. His prayer in that extreme condition is: 'I do not desire from God the highest powers. I do not even want liberation. What I want is only this: That I am able to go and live in the hearts of all beings and undergo sufferings on their behalf, so that they may become free from all miseries.'

A common theme in most of the Puranic stories is that God protects His devotees. God is also all-powerful and destroys evil and ensures that good prevails. Many Puranas have a section devoted to Devi worship, i.e., of the feminine aspect of God. The Markandeya Purana, one of the most ancient, has the famous Devi Mahatmyam or the Chandi. This is regarded as a sacred text and is chanted today whenever the Mother Goddess is worshipped. Some chant it regularly as part of their devotional practices. The Goddess is all-powerful and destroys evil, for instance in the form of the demon Mahishasura. She is also kind and benevolent and bestows wealth as Lakshmi and knowledge as Saraswati.

The Puranas follow the fivefold attributes or *Panchalakshanas* namely *sarga* (cosmogony or the origin of the universe), *pratisarga* (cosmology or the study of the cosmos), *vamsa* (genealogy of gods, sages and kings), *manvantara* (the study of cosmic cycles) and *vamsanucharitram* (the legends of the times of various kings). Some Puranas include additional sections called *Mahatmyas* (literally, 'greatness of something') and even tour guides to places of pilgrimage. All the Puranas are attributed to the sage, Veda Vyasa. Since the Puranas span millennia, it is clear that 'Vyasa' is just a generic name. It may have been a practice for authors not to claim credit for themselves, instead using 'Vyasa'. This may have increased the acceptance and credibility of the text.

The Puranas have a much wider influence on the practice of Hinduism than the more revered texts such as the Vedas, Upanishads and the Gita. There are so many myths, legends and stories that are popular with people and can easily be understood. The Puranas also humanize God, making it easier to worship and access Him. In a philosophical sense, the Puranas are largely dualistic where God and man are separate. Man prays to God who, in turn, protects him, and bestows happiness and other rewards. However, there are many passages that are highly philosophical as well. A comprehensive and detailed description of the Puranas is an almost impossible task.

Summary and Some Notes

The Puranas came after the Vedas and evolved over centuries. They are largely about devotion to God. Collectively they are more voluminous than the Vedas. While there are some philosophical sections, it is largely about cosmogony (origin of the Universe), cosmology, gods, myths, stories, kings and sacred places. The mythological stories about various gods are very popular even today. In contrast to the Upanishadic concept of a formless, attribute-less Supreme Reality called Brahman, the Puranas are about Personal Gods with form and attributes. This has a great appeal to seekers and religious persons who have devotion to God. The Puranas have also helped the ideas in the Vedas and the Upanishads to spread among the masses. Popular Hinduism is based on the Puranas.

The Puranas also highlight some of the unique aspects of Hinduism. There are multiple gods and an individual can worship any of the various gods based on his or her temperament. In practice, religious Hindus visit the temples of various gods and goddesses. A careful reading of the Puranas also reveals that all these gods are manifestations of the One Supreme Reality, namely Brahman. You can reach that goal by worship of any of the gods. You can also directly approach the Ultimate Reality. This is unique to Hinduism as other major religions are monotheistic with One God and a single founder. The concept of the '*avatar*' or the descent of God in human form is also unique. Unlike Christianity where there is only one Incarnation, Hinduism says there can be many Incarnations.

8

AGAMA SASTRAS

The word 'agama' in Sanskrit literally means 'that which has come'. By implication and common understanding, it means ancient knowledge that has been handed down to future generations. According to another interpretation, agama refers to that which has descended from above. There is no clear consensus on when the Agama Sastras were written. Some of the earliest references to what later became known as Saivism and Vaishnavism are found in the Mahabharata, which is dated prior to the time of the Buddha. It is more than likely that the ideas we find in the fully developed Agama texts existed much earlier. The texts themselves were probably written over the course of a few centuries.[1]

The most influential texts are the Vaishnava Agamas, the Saiva Agamas and the Sakti Agamas which are also known as the Tantra. Scholars, however, apply the word Tantra to several other texts as well as to the Saiva and Vaishnava Agamas. For instance, Adi Sankara uses the term 'Sankhya tantra' to refer to the Sankhya philosophy. The word 'tantra' is sometimes defined as tanyate vistaryate jnanam anena iti tantram or 'that which spreads knowledge is tantra'. According to some classifications, there are twenty-eight Saiva Agama texts, seventy-seven Sakti or Tantra texts and 108 Vaishnava Agama texts. However, other classifications assign different numbers. Practitioners of the two other tantras—one based on Ganapati, the elephant-headed God and the other on Surya, the Sun God—are much less prevalent today. However, beyond the tantra, worship of Ganapati is widespread throughout the country even today. Some of the well-known texts include the Pancharatra for the Vaishanavas and the Mahanirvana Tantra for the Saktas.[2]

The tantras or Agamas also have emancipation or liberation of the individual as the goal. They also in general accept the authority of the Vedas. Some say that the four eras or ages are for different scriptures. The Vedas are for the most ancient Satya Yuga (the Age of Truth), the Smritis for the Treta Yuga (which is when the incarnation of Rama took place), the Puranas for the Dvapara Yuga (incarnation of Krishna) and the Tantra for the present Kali Yuga.* The Agamas claim that they are also revelatory and therefore are Shruti. Since they accept the Vedas, they are also

---

* In a similar vein, the different Smritis giving the Dharma or the Law also are said to be relevant for different yugas or eras.

regarded as scripture. For instance, the Kulavarna Tantra, the Prapancasara Tantra, the Matsyasukta Mahatantra and the Gandharva Tantra all accept the Vedas and say that the Vedas are supreme. They say that the follower of the Agama path must be a pure soul who has studied the Vedas. Some say that the Tantras are the fifth Veda, although a similar claim is made for the Puranas and the Mahabharata also.

The *tantra* has influenced popular Hinduism considerably. The lofty philosophical and contemplative methods of the Upanishads are replaced with methods that are accessible to everyone. The Agama Sastras place no restriction on caste or gender. The Gautamiya Tantra says

Sarva varnadhikaras cha
Narinam yogya eva cha

This is translated as 'All castes are eligible, and women as well.'

This is in contrast to some of the Vedic rites where caste and gender rules were introduced, possibly in later times. Some scholars say that both the Vedic and Agama traditions co-existed even during ancient times.

Perhaps the great insight in the *tantra* is that for the vast majority of people, a life of complete renunciation is neither possible nor desirable. The *tantra* finds a way for all, irrespective of gender and caste. Acceptance of the world and fulfilling desires according to *dharma* is accepted. This is in contrast to the approach of the Upanishads which emphasizes renunciation. The Agama scriptures guide the individual, beginning from where they are and lead them to higher levels, not by external renunciation but by advocating proper enjoyment of the world and then going beyond it. The Agama practices accept that the world is real and that the senses provide delight and in practice do not shun the worldly life. Yet, by proper regulation, they give a higher turn to life and help the individual to progress towards God.* The Karma Kanda of the Vedas also does not shun this world and has *kamya karmas*, or rituals with desire. However, the actual Agama and Vedic rituals are quite different.

In general, the Agamas have a *jnana pada* or a section dedicated to knowledge which describes the philosophy. The *yoga pada* mentions the practices that lead to higher states of consciousness, the *kriya pada* lays down details for esoteric† rituals and the *charya pada* lists the rules for conduct of external worship.

Although the Agamas have different philosophies, all of them accept that there is a non-material soul that is essentially divine and that the purpose of life is its realization. However, the Supreme is regarded variously as

---

* In modern times, sages such as Sri Ramakrishna endorsed some of the Tantric practices.
† Refers to practices given to the disciple by the teacher or *guru*.

Siva, Vishnu or Sakti, the Divine Mother. The *yoga pada* is largely based on concentration. However it also includes worshipping God as defined by that Agama. The inner aspects of the Agama practices link the individual, the mind and the senses to the divine. Externally, it has rituals, symbols, worship, idols and temples. Devotion is a central aspect in the practices.

A major departure from the Vedic rituals is the use of idols and their worship. Vedic rituals do not require idols or temples. They are based on invoking the formless *devas* or gods usually through *agni* or fire. However, the Agamas sanction the worship of God through idols. Many of the rituals performed in temples follow one or the other of the Agama texts. They also contain rules about the worship of other gods like Ganesha, Surya and Skanda (the younger son of Siva). Even when seeking liberation, the Agama Sastras allow worship of God with form unlike the Upanishads which do not mention any idol worship.

Three Major Branches of the Agama Sastras

The Vaishnava Agamas focus on Vishnu as the Supreme God. However, Vaishnavism as prevalent today evolved from the Agama Sastras as well as from later philosophies and the teachings of *gurus*. The Pancharatra is a major Agama text. According to this text, God exists and we can perceive Him in in five ways. These are transcendent, manifest, as incarnation, as idol and as the indwelling God in each one of us.[*]

As *para*, God is identified with Narayana or Vishnu. God has six major attributes—*jnana* or knowledge, *aisvarya* or lordship (over the universe), *sakti* or omnipotence, *bala* or strength, *virya* or virility and *tejas* or splendour. This God is the Ultimate Reality. As *vyuha* (which emanates from the *para*), God is manifested as Vasudeva, Sankarshana, Pradyumna and Aniruddha. Vasudeva is the supreme manifestation and is usually considered to be Krishna. Sankarshana is Balarama, his elder brother. Pradyumna and Aniruddha are Krishna's son and grandson respectively. Each of these aspects has a religious and metaphysical significance. As *vaibhava* or incarnation, God has ten *avatars*: Matsya (fish), Kurma (tortoise), Varaha (boar), Narasimha (man-lion), Vamana (dwarf), Parasurama, Rama, Balarama, Krishna and Kalki.[†] Kalki, the final *avatar*, is yet to be manifested. As *archa* or idol, God becomes easy to approach. When the proper rites are followed, the Divine enters into the idol for the benefit of the devotees.[‡] According to

---

[*] *Para, vyuha, vaibhava, archa* and *antaryamin* respectively.

[†] Some Puranas replace Balarama with Buddha whereas others mention twenty-four *avatars* or Incarnations. However, in the Vaishnava Agamas, all the *avatars* are of Vishnu.

[‡] God's presence in the idol is invoked after performing the proper *puja* and rituals and the idol is said to be awakened or *jagrut*.

some, the idol is the most accessible of the five forms of God. In practice, this is true as large numbers of people visit temples daily. The Vaishnava Agamas originally sought to break the barriers of caste, creed and gender in worship. Vaishnavism, which developed from these texts, also accepts supremacy of the Vedas. They use Sanskrit texts especially the Agama and the Bhagavata Purana and also use local languages. This helped to make it popular and disseminate it in different regions. As *antaryamin*, God resides in every individual and can be sought by the devotee internally as well.

The Saiva Agama texts are less ritualistic. *Pati* or Siva is the Supreme Being and *pashu* or animal is the individual. The animal tendencies or *pasha* bind the individual. Another name for Siva is Pashupati, the Lord of All Beings. Worship of Siva eventually overcomes all animal tendencies in us. They describe eight qualities of Siva which are independence, purity, self-knowledge, omniscience, freedom from defilement, boundless benevolence, omnipotence and bliss. The philosophy developed in Kashmir and as Saiva Siddhanta in Tamil Nadu. Saivism accepts both the Vedas and the Agama Sastras. Both Sanskrit and local languages are used in these texts as well making them popular with a large number of people. While there are innumerable temples dedicated to Siva, all of them may not follow the Agama rituals and texts.

The Agama Sastras do not completely define Vaishnavism and Saivism as practiced today. The two evolved not only from the Agamas, but also from the Vedas, Puranas, and local practices.

The Sakti Agama texts are generally referred to as *tantra*. It refers to the manifest God, especially as 'sakti' or 'energy' which is the Divine Mother. Kashmir Saivism, though not a part of the Sakta Agamas, is very similar and says that everything is One though it appears as two—manifest and unmanifest, matter and soul, still and moving, male and female and so on. The primeval spiritual union of the two leads to the highest bliss. The difference is in emphasizing Siva or Sakti. Unlike philosophies such as the Advaita which say that nothing except Brahman is real, the Sakti Agamas say that the world is real. Tantra says that the manifest world is not evil, that desires need to be understood and one can go beyond them by satisfying them in the proper way. They describe different states of the spiritual seeker. Early-stage seekers are those whose animal propensities are strong. They are known as 'pasu'. The next higher stage is for the normal human being, sometimes known as 'vira' or hero. The third stage is for the 'divya', those in whom the divine element is prominent. The Tantric practices are classified into Vedachara, Vaishnavachara, Saivachara, Dakshanachara, Vamachara, Siddhantachara and Kaulachara. The first three are identified with the *pasu* or the animal stage, the next two with the heroic stage and the last two with the divine stage of the individual. Worship of the Divine as a Goddess is very prominent in Tantra. This aspect is very popular all over India with numerous temples to the Divine in the form of various goddesses.

There is also an inner or esoteric aspect to the Agama Sastras. They refer to *mantra, yantra* and *tantra. Mantra* refers to the use of mystic syllables which are usually handed down even today from teacher to disciple. Initiation into a *mantra* by a competent *guru* helps the seeker to move faster towards the goal of life. The Vedas and Upanishads only mention the importance of the sacred word and identify it with 'Om' which is said to be the same as Brahman. There are a few other well-known *mantras* in the Vedas such as the Gayatri Mantra. The Agama *mantras*, however, are about a specific God. Some are well known such as 'Om namo Narayanaya' and 'Om namah Sivaya'. They refer to Vishnu or Narayana and Siva respectively. They mean Om, (I) salute Narayana and Om (I) Salute Siva. There are several *mantras* for various aspects of God, and the tantra in particular has *mantras* invoking the Mother Goddess or Sakti in various forms. *Yantra* refers to mystical diagrams that are used for conducting rituals. The Sakti, Vaishnava and Saiva Agamas have such diagrams. These are used along with the *mantras* and are considered to be powerful methods for the advanced spiritual seeker. They are also said to lead to powers of the mind like memory, clairvoyance and so on. However, there is a warning that without instruction from a competent *guru*, purity of mind, good character, and giving up selfish desires, these practices can lead to a fall for the spiritual aspirant. However, when properly used they can lead the individual to higher levels.

In a certain sense, the popular religion we see today is directly or indirectly influenced by the Agama Sastras and their development into Vaishnavism, Shaivism and Sakti worship. Temple construction, ritual and worship are also based on these texts. Along with the Puranas, the Ramayana and the Mahabharata, they were often used as the basis for creating literature, poems, songs and rituals in local languages.

Summary

The Agama Sastras, sometimes referred to as the *tantra*, are based on some key assumptions or insights. In other traditions like the Upanishads, the spiritual aspirant is asked to renounce all worldly joys. Tantra recognizes that the overwhelming majority of people cannot do that. At the same time there are many who are genuine spiritual aspirants. So it accepts the world as real and not as something to be renounced. Worship of one's Ishta or Personal God (Vishnu, Siva or the Divine Mother) is suitable for many people. The Agama Sastras also prescribe the proper rituals, symbols and *mantras* for such worship.

Temples are built and worship is performed using the rules laid down in these texts.

The three major Agama Sastras are also based on certain basic insights into the human mind. One set of people view the world as real and God as immanent in the universe. Vishnu is the immanent God that pervades everything. For another set of people, the world is no doubt real, but the Ultimate Reality is transcendent. Siva is the transcendent God. For yet another set of people, God is Power. The Divine Mother is all powerful and is called *Sakti*, or power. Perhaps the three Agamas evolved to suit different temperaments.

Tantra also discovered that through legitimate enjoyment,* one can transcend earthly desire and progress towards the goal of spiritual life. In practice, this is usually very difficult to achieve as most people who follow tantra are then unable to rise above their desires. However, done in the proper manner, with the right attitude and under the guidance of a *guru*, liberation is possible. In recent times, Sri Ramakrishna practiced all the Tantric disciplines and concluded that they are all valid means for spiritual aspirants. While a popular perception is that Tantra is only about sensual enjoyment, the texts themselves are

---

* Krishna in the Gita gives a similar teaching. 'I am the desire in all beings that is not opposed to virtue—*dharma-aviruddho bhuteshu kamasmi.*

quite different. They present a comprehensive method for spiritual aspirants and gradually take them beyond the satisfaction of legitimate desires towards the ultimate goal of life.

9

OTHER SACRED TEXTS

There are other ancient texts which are significant. They are briefly discussed in this chapter as they are considered to be sacred and important. One set of these texts are supplementary to the Vedas. A second set of texts are the Smritis. Though the term 'Smriti' refers to several later texts, here only those that are explicitly called Smriti, e.g., the Manu Smriti, are discussed. The third set of texts includes philosophical treatises based on the Upanishads and is studied by serious spiritual seekers.

Texts Supplementary to the Vedas

The Upavedas and the Vedangas are considered to be auxiliary or supplementary to the Vedas. There are four Upavedas pertaining to the sciences and arts—Sthapatyaveda (on architecture) in the Rig Veda, Dhanurveda (archery) in the Yajur Veda, Gandharvaveda (music and sacred dance) in the Sama Veda and Ayurveda (medicine) in the Atharva

Veda. Temples are often built using the principles laid down in the Sthapatyaveda. Those well-versed in this are called Sthapatis and are called upon to build temples even today. When the Vedas were composed, archery was the principal means of hunting and warfare. The Ramayana and Mahabharata are full of incidents where archery is used in war. Classical music and dance in India developed from the Gandharvaveda. '*Ayurveda*' literally means 'the knowledge of (long) life' and is the science of well-being and health. Ayurvedic treatment and medicines are frequently used in India and Ayurvedic practices are being researched using modern scientific knowledge. They are now considered as secular subjects, but perhaps in those days, knowledge was regarded as one and included in the sacred texts.

'*Vedanga*' literally means 'the parts or limbs of the Vedas'. They tell us how to read the Vedas and the rules according to which they were revealed. The six subjects covered by them include phonetics or *siksha*, rules of poetry and metre or *chandas*, grammar or *vyakarana*, linguistics or *nirukta,* rituals and rites of passage of an individual's life or *kalpa* and astrology or *jyotisha*. *Siksha* tells us how to pronounce and properly chant the Vedic hymns and *mantras*. This is a precise method, although there are a few schools that follow their own distinct style of chanting. The Vedic hymns and many of the later sacred verses are composed using the rules of *chandas*. Sanskrit grammar or *vyakarana* is highly evolved. *Nirukta* is concerned with etymology or the root of words and their proper meaning. The *kalpa sutras* describe the rituals and rites of passage including birth, the first feeding of solid food to the child, the beginning of education, the completion of education, marriage and death. *Jyotisha* or astrology was also highly developed and has parallels with western astrology.

The Smritis

The word '*smriti*' means 'that which is remembered'. The Smritis do not have the status of the Upanishads. In some classifications, all later texts are included in the term 'Smriti'. These include the Vedangas, Upavedas, the Itihasas, the Puranas and so on. Here we limit ourselves to the texts which are explicitly called Smritis and offer a brief introduction to their principal ideas.

There are eighteen major Smritis.* The well-known ones are the Manu, Yajnavalkya and Parasara Smritis. There is another list of Upasmritis or minor Smritis, most of which are very voluminous. Though based on Vedanta, the Smritis are more practical and discuss topics related

---

* The most widely accepted list of major Smritis is Angirasa, Vyasa, Apastamba, Daksha, Vishnu, Yagnavalkya, Likhita, Samvarta, Shankha, Brihaspati, Atri, Katyayana, Parasara, Manu, Ausanasi, Harita, Gautama and Yama. Some lists also include the Satapata and Vasishtha Smritis.

to day-to-day life, conduct, behaviour, ethics, morals, *dharma*, role of the individual in society and so on. Serious spiritual seekers usually do not study them.

These texts are also called the Dharma Sastras, texts that describe the laws and rules that guide individuals and communities in their daily conduct. '*Dharma*' is derived from the root word '*dhr*' which means 'that which holds or supports'. *Dharma* in this sense refers to the law that holds together our conduct. However, in daily usage, the word is used in a variety of contexts and does not have a precise meaning. All the Smritis defer to the Vedas. Unlike the Vedas and Upanishads that contain eternal truths based on direct revelation, the Smritis are regarded as relevant for particular times. For instance, there is a Sanskrit verse which says that the Laws of Manu are relevant for the *Krta Yuga* or the Vedic Age, those of Yajnavalkya Smirit for the *Treta Yuga* during the time of the Ramayana, those of the Likhita Smriti for the *Dvapara Yuga* during the time of the Mahabharata and those of the Parasara Smriti for the *Kali Yuga* or the present age. It is also accepted that whenever there is a contradiction between the Vedas and any other text including the Smritis, the authority of the Vedas prevails.

The Manu Smriti is known as the *Manava Dharmashastra*. Its precise date of composition is uncertain, with some scholars placing it as early as 1000 BCE while others suggest a date as late as 200 BCE. It was by Manu with some parts attributed to another sage, Bhrigu. There are various versions of the text and it is difficult to say what was original and what was later interpolated. It has twelve chapters and about 2700 verses. It deals with cosmogony or the origin of the universe, *dharma* or the proper way of life and conduct, the *samskaras* or rituals like the sacred thread ceremony, marriage, funeral rites, pollution and purification. It is concerned with the conduct of ordinary people as well as rulers. It also lays down a law without distinguishing between religious and secular. It discusses rules governing charity and other good actions, *karma* and liberation. For instance, it extols virtues such as non-injury, truth, compassion, forbearance, self-control, charity, self-restraint, moderation and so on. Nearly half the verses deal with the conduct of Brahmins, and another third with that of Kshatriyas or the warrior class. Only a small part is devoted to the conduct of the other two *varnas* (nowadays loosely translated as caste) called Vaishya and Shudra. It is not clear whether these *varnas* were based on the family in which one was born, or determined by temperament. It encourages people to be vegetarian and refrain from liquor, but it is not a strict injunction. Rules for war say that non-combatants, civilians, women and those who surrender should not be harmed. There are even rules for taxation and are aimed at the rulers.

Since there are many versions of the Manu Smriti, there are a few inconsistencies. It extols the position of women, and says that a society that does not honour and respect women will be ruined. It also gives a status to women that by modern standards is inferior. It also assigns an inferior status to Shudras. It is unlikely that the Manu Smriti was ever introduced by any king as the law. In modern times, the text has attracted both praise and condemnation. In particular, the portions that deal with the status of women and the so-called 'lower castes' have been criticized. The Manu Smriti's impact on Hindu religion that relates man to God or to the Ultimate Reality is minimal.

The Yajnavalkya Smriti is named after the famous sage Yajnavalkya who gives the teaching in the Brihadaranyaka Upanishad. But since the Smriti comes several centuries later, it was attributed to him. This was a tradition in those times, and many texts spanning centuries are attributed to a respected name. The Yajnavalkya Smriti is shorter and deals with *achara* or conduct, *vyavahara* or legal laws and conduct and *prayaschitta* or penance. It says, for instance, that loan agreements should be written down and entered into with mutual consent. It also says that a woman should be respected by everyone in the household. The texts are written in a systematic way.

The texts that are explicitly called Smriti are not only about God or metaphysics. They contain guidelines about day-to-day life, conduct, and morals and outline the role of different sections of society. They are said to be contextual truths rather than eternal truths. As times change, the

Smritis relevant to that particular age also change. Some modern-day scholars say that the world has changed so much over the past millennia that there may be a need for a new Smriti as some of the older ones may no longer be relevant or valid.

Others also quote from the Smritis to say that those of good character can be guided by their conscience. This is even higher than the Smriti.

Other Ancient Philosophical Texts

This is another set of texts that are considered important. We describe briefly the *sutras*, and three ancient treatises that discuss through story and dialogue the subtle philosophies and truths in the Upanishads, namely the Tripura Rahasya, the Yoga Vasishtha and the Adhyatma Ramayana; There are also various other sacred texts that are called 'Gita' which are also briefly discussed.

The *sutras* Literature

Some religious texts are written in concise phrases or aphorisms (a short statement that contains a deeper truth). This is in the *sutra* style of writing. The word *sutra* means string or thread. The most famous *sutra* text is the Brahma Sutra. Buddhist texts also use this format and are called *suttas* while Jain texts call them *suyas*. They are distilled statements around which commentaries and discussions often take place. Some of the *darsanas* are also called *sutras*, such as the Nyaya, Vaiseshika, Sankhya, Yoga and Mimamsa Sutras. A typical example of a *sutra* from the Yoga Sutras is '*Yoga chitta vritti nirodha*', or '*Yoga* is the control of the *vrittis* or modifications of the *chitta* or mind stuff'. This is an aphorism and has been explained at length by commentators. It goes into questions like what Yoga is, what is meant by the mind, what are the modifications in the mind, why do we need to control the mind and so on. All the texts known as *sutras* are written in a similar style.

One of the well-known *sutras* is the Narada Bhakti Sutras which is to be distinguished from the Narada Purana. This is a treatise on *bhakti* or devotion. The Narada Bhakti Sutras are very short and contain only eighty-four verses organized into chapters. It begins by defining what *bhakti* is and then says that self-surrender and renunciation are prerequisites for attaining true *bhakti*. It recounts the greatness of ancient devotees. It endorses *bhakti* as a desirable goal of life and offers suggestions about how to attain this, and exhorts us to seek holy company. It talks of different grades of *bhakti* and divine love. It has some practices including worship of God and emphasizes the need for proper conduct. Although it has only seventy-seven verses, the Siva Sutras by Vasugupta constitute the foundation of Kashmir Saivism. There are *sutra*-like verses in the Vedas as well.

The Dattatreya Tradition and the Tripura Rahasya

There are three highly regarded texts which are considered highly philosophical and explain the Upanishadic Truths through stories and dialogue. Unlike the Puranas which are about Personal Gods and devotion, these texts guide the seeker to the Formless Reality of Brahman. However, they accept some amount of ritual and symbols as means to the goal. They are briefly discussed here because serious spiritual seekers study them even today. Some of the modern sages and teachers also refer to them in their teachings.

One of these texts is based on Dattatreya who contains within himself the holy trinity of Brahma, Siva and Narayana or Vishnu. He is the Teacher of Teachers and of *Avadhutas*, a special class of illumined persons who are beyond all social norms and conventions. Dattatreya is depicted with three heads representing Brahma, Siva and Vishnu. In front of him are four black dogs which represent the Vedas. He has six hands with the symbols of Vishnu, Siva and Brahma. These are the conch or *sankha,* and the disc or *chakra* of Vishnu, the drum or *damaru* and the trident *trishul* of Siva, and the rosary *aksharamala* and water pot *kamandalu* of Brahma. A cow is also depicted and denotes the universe. The symbolism of the four dogs is unmistakable: for the enlightened sage, the sacred texts have no meaning as he has gone beyond them. Dattatreya is the teacher in the Tripura Rahasya as well as in the Avadhuta Gita.

In the Tripura Rahasya, Dattatreya reveals the teaching to Parasurama, one of the ten *avatars* or Incarnations. It is extremely lengthy and has more than 12,000 verses. It tells the well-known story of the King Hemachuda who was looking for spiritual truth. His wife, Hemalekha, an illumined sage herself, teaches him the divine knowledge. After performing penance, the king also becomes illumined and then continues to rule his kingdom. The meaning of the term '*tripura rahasya*' is 'three secrets' or 'mysteries'. Here, '*tripura*' refers to the three states of waking, dreaming and deep sleep. The secret behind them is Consciousness, otherwise known as the *turiya* state which permeates all the other three states. Abiding in the *turiya* state is liberation. This basic exposition is there in the Upanishads as well, particularly the Mandukya. In the Tripura Rahasya, this is developed in much greater detail in a human context. It has three sections. The first section is called the Jnana Kanda or knowledge section, the second is called the Mahatmya Kanda and is about the greatness of the Divine Mother or Goddess and the final section is called the Charya Kanda or the section on conduct. It discusses the various impediments to enlightenment as well as the methods of gaining it.

The Yoga Vasishtha and Adhyatma Ramayana

The Yoga Vasishtha is based on the Ramayana, although it was written much later. Scholars disagree on the precise date of composition but say it was written after the 6th century ce. It is also known as the Maha Ramayana, Uttara Ramayana and Vasishtha Ramayana. The text is based on the teaching given by the sage, Vasishtha to his young disciple, Rama of the Ramayana. The *laghu* Ramayana is a shorter spiritual version with about 6000 verses. The longer version of the Yoga Vasishtha has over 30,000 verses. It is attributed to Valmiki, the original author of the Ramayana, but appears as instructions given by Vasishtha. Rama is struck by the futility and misery of existence and wants to renounce the world. Vasishtha then teaches him spiritual knowledge. He also makes Rama reflect that everything is Brahman and the world is also part of the same reality. So where will he go? Rama reflects and accepts this truth. This text is held in high esteem by serious spiritual seekers as it gives the highest teachings in a simple way. Interestingly, this also contains a lengthy story about a royal couple like the Tripura Rahasya. In this story, the queen Chudala is once again the *guru* for her husband Sikidwaja and guides him towards self-realization.

Another text which was written much later is the Adhyatma Ramayana. This text follows the original Valmiki Ramayana but gives it a completely spiritual meaning. '*Adhyatma*' means the supreme Self or Atman. The text says that Rama is a Divine incarnation and gives several spiritual teachings. It follows the Vedantic teachings and gives them in simpler poetical form, often in the form of dialogues. Here Rama is the teacher, whereas in the Yoga Vasishtha he is the disciple. The Adhyatma Ramayana contains the Rama Gita, a short text of sixty highly philosophical verses.

The Various Gitas

Like the two texts based on the Ramayana, there are several texts that go by the name of 'Gita'. The most famous and revered is the Bhagavad Gita. However, there are others as well. The Anu Gita was narrated a second time by Krishna to Arjuna after the war when the Pandavas had established their kingdom. The Uddhava Gita was taught by Krishna to his friend Uddhava. The Vyadha Gita is based on an interesting story. A young *yogi* was meditating under a tree and was displeased when a crow on a branch above defecated on him. He looked up in anger and the crow was reduced to ashes. Somewhat pleased that he had gained *yogic* powers, he went to collect alms. The lady of the house makes him wait as she attends to her aged father and mother-in-law, husband and other family members. She finally comes and gives him alms but says, 'I am not a crow that will be reduced to ashes.' The *yogi* is surprised and learns that she got all this wisdom merely by doing her duty. When he wants to learn more, she sends him to meet her *guru*. After travelling a long distance, he locates *him* in the butcher's shop. He is aghast to see a butcher as the *guru*. The *vyadha* or butcher also makes him wait till he finishes his duties. The *yogi*, who had been suitably chastened by the lady, waited patiently. The teaching provided by the butcher is called the Vyadha Gita. The Guru Gita is a part of the Skanda Purana and is a teaching given by Siva to his consort, Parvati. The Ganesh Gita is taught by the elephant-headed god, Ganesh or Gajanana to a king. The Ribhu Gita was taught by Lord Siva to the sage Ribhu in Mount Kailash in the Himalayas. The Ashtavakra Gita also called the Ashtavakra Samhita was taught by a sage of the same name to Janaka, a king. '*Ashtavakra*' means 'one with eight deformities' and describes the eight defects in the body of the teacher. The Avadhuta Gita is a song of freedom sung by Dattatreya. The Moksha Gita gives teachings about gaining liberation or *moksha*. In addition to these, there are several other texts that also use the word 'Gita'.

Summary

The Upavedas and Vedanga are not regarded as spiritual texts. The former discusses science and the arts whereas the latter lays down rules of grammar, poetry and ancillary subjects that are found in the Vedas. The Smritis were written down at the time of composition unlike the earlier texts which came down through oral traditions. They are more about rules of conduct, morals, ethics and how society should be organized. Their relevance is specific to their time of composition and they are usually regarded as secondary in importance to the Vedas.

Among the spiritual texts, the *sutras* like the Narada Bhakti Sutras are important basic texts laying down a philosophy for the Bhakti tradition. The Tripura Rahasya, the Yoga Vasishtha and the Adhyatma Ramayana are long and elaborate texts containing many stories and lengthy dialogues which present the Vedantic teachings in a more accessible way. The various Gitas are about the ultimate reality, the nature of man, and the methods of realizing Brahman. Based essentially on Vedanta, they are held in high esteem and are used by spiritual seekers for guidance.

10

THE ITIHASAS OR EPICS

The word 'Itihasa' literally means 'history'. The two sacred texts classified as 'Itihasa' are the well-known epics, the Ramayana and the Mahabharata. They are popular even today and Indians are generally aware of the important events that are a part of these epics. During the medieval period, they were translated from Sanskrit into various Indian languages. They have also been translated into several European languages. Reciting them is considered a part of regular worship. The Ramayana is recited over several days in congregations. The Mahabharata contains the Bhagavad Gita, the Vishnu *Sahasranama*, the thousand names of Vishnu and other sacred texts that are recited even today.*

---

* The *Vishnu Sahasranama* is also found in other texts like the Padma Purana, the Garuda Purana and the Skanda Purana.

The Ramayana

The Ramayana has about 24,000 verses in what is called the *anushtuba* metre of poetry. It was composed by the sage, Valmiki who was a hunter. He underwent a transformation and then composed the epic. The epic is divided into seven parts or '*kandas*'. Some scholars believe that the first and last *kanda* were added later. The Ramayana is about the life of Rama, one of the incarnations of God. It is set in the *Treta Yuga* or the era which succeeded the *Satya Yuga* or the *Krita Yuga* of the Vedas. It is considered more ancient than the Mahabharata. The story begins with Dasaratha, the king and father of Rama and his brothers. He desired virtuous progeny and performed the Putra Kameshti *yajna*, the sacrifice performed for the birth of sons. He had four sons through his three wives. Rama was the son of Kausalya, Lakshmana and his twin Shatrughna were born to Sumitra and Bharata to Kaikeyi. The story describes the childhood and youth of the brothers. They were trained by competent *gurus* including Viswamitra and Vasishtha. They learnt all that was required of a prince including such skills as archery, warfare, philosophy, how to govern and so on. It describes how Rama was so skilled that he could defeat anyone and protected the sages who were tormented by *asuras* or demons. He defeated all of them. He then married Sita, the daughter of king Janaka. Janaka wanted Sita to marry the prince who could string Pinaka, the bow of Siva. Rama strings it and breaks the bow thus winning the hand of Sita.

As preparations were going on for Rama's coronation as the prince who would succeed Dasaratha, the story takes a turn. Kaikeyi, one of Dasaratha's wives, is influenced by her maid, Manthara and demands that her son, Bharata be crowned instead. Manthara was worried that Kaikeyi would lose her status as a favourite queen if Rama became king. She reminds her of a promise given by Dasaratha to Kaikeyi that he would grant her two boons. She is finally persuaded by Manthara. Kaikeyi demands that Bharata be coronated and Rama be sent into exile for fourteen years. Dasaratha is devastated but is a man of his word. Rama also cheerfully tells his father that he should follow the *dharma* and accept Kaikeyi's demands. He goes into exile accompanied by his wife, Sita and his brother Lakshmana. Dasaratha dies of grief. This event is interpreted as the need to follow the Truth and keep one's promise, even renouncing one's kingdom if required. The ideal son obeys his virtuous father. It lays down the *dharma*.

A major part of the epic depicts life in the forests. The hardships they face, the sages they meet, and the demons they had to fight to protect the sages. The story takes another turn when Surpanakha, the sister of the highly powerful and gifted king Ravana of Lanka (present-day Sri Lanka), comes across the two brothers. She makes amorous advances repeatedly, and to send her away once and for all,

Lakshmana cuts off her nose. She goes back to her brother in pain and humiliation. Ravana is enraged and decides to take revenge. He entices the demon Maricha to take the form of a golden deer. Sita is fascinated by it and asks Rama to hunt it for her. He goes reluctantly and leaves his brother Lakshmana to protect her. Rama succeeds in killing the deer, but as planned, Maricha while dying, lets out a wail, 'Oh! Lakshmana'. Sita hears it and thinks it is Rama calling for help. She asks Lakshmana to go and help Rama who she thinks is in danger. Lakshmana is reluctant and argues that Rama is all-powerful and cannot be harmed, but Sita persists. Lakshmana agrees to go out in search of Rama, but to pre-empt any danger to Sita's life, he draws a line around the hut and tells her that as long as she was within it, she was safe. This is the *Lakshmana Rekha* or Lakshmana's line.* It is part of common language today and is used to convey the limits of legitimate action. Crossing the line is not acceptable. Ravana, who was waiting for Lakshmana to leave, approaches Sita in the guise of a *sannyasi*. He asks for alms and persuades her to cross the Lakshmana Rekha. He says that as a *sannyasi* he cannot enter a household. As soon she does, he seizes her and takes her on his flying vehicle to Lanka crossing the ocean.

Rama and Lakshmana are distraught to find Sita missing and start searching for her. The items that she had

---

* The Rekha is not there in the Valmiki Ramayana but is part of popular folklore.

discarded from the chariot offer some clues. The search for Sita brings Rama in touch with Sugriva who becomes his friend. He is the king of the *vanaras*. This is usually meant to mean the monkeys, but some say it could refer in the language of those days to indigenous or tribal people living in the forests. They come across the dying bird Jatayu who fought bravely with Ravana in the sky to save Sita. They come to know that she was taken to Lanka. Hanuman the loyal devotee of Rama is sent to Lanka. He is afraid of crossing the ocean, but is egged on by Jambavan, the wise king of bears, and in one giant leap he flies across to Lanka. 'Hanuman's leap' is also a part of common language today and refers to a great or outstanding feat. The phrase is also used to encourage an individual to take a bold step or action like Hanuman. In Lanka, Hanuman sees Sita as well as the splendour and might of Ravana and his kingdom. He covertly shows her the earrings she had discarded and convinces her that he had indeed been sent by Rama. He wants to take her back over the ocean but Sita refuses, saying that she wants Rama to have the glory of victory and of rescuing her. After a few adventures, Hanuman once again crosses the ocean and returns to Rama.

Rama decides to go to Lanka and rescue Sita. Accompanied by Lakshmana, Sugriva and the army of monkeys, they reach a southern tip of India, now called Rameswaram and build a bridge. This bridge today is called Dhanushkoti. They cross over to Lanka and an epic war ensues in which Ravana, his brother Kumbhakarana and his sons, including Indrajit, are killed. The text has descriptions of various battles, use of celestial weapons, the might of both armies, and the strength, valour and skill of various warriors. It even has a glowing description of Ravana who is praised as a great warrior. However, he is ultimately killed by Rama and Sita is rescued. According to the norms of the times, she has to prove her chastity and purity by undergoing a fire ordeal. She comes out unscathed. Rama then returns with everyone and makes his way back to Ayodhya. By this time the period of exile is over. His brother Bharata is also extremely pleased and gladly hands over the kingdom to Rama.

According to some scholars, the original Valmiki Ramayana ends with the return to Ayodhya, and the final section or Uttara Kanda was added later. Rama rules Ayodhya and establishes *Rama Rajya* or the ideal kingdom. However, after some time, Sita is once again put to a test on the complaint of a washerman. Apparently, a woman who lived in another man's house was not fit to be a queen. Although there had been no relationship between Sita and Ravana, many people refused to accept her as the queen. Consequently, Sita is banished from the kingdom. Rama follows the King's *dharma* of those days but is grief stricken. Sita takes refuge in the hermitage of the Sage Valmiki. She was pregnant when she was banished, and gives birth to the twins Luva and Kusha.

Rama performs the Ashvamedha *yajna** to establish his empire over large regions. At the concluding ceremony, Luva and Kusha appear and narrate the entire story of the Ramayana. Realizing that they are his sons, Rama asks Sita to return. She does, but is again asked to take a test to prove her chastity and purity. Tired of being subjected to the repeated humiliation of proving her chastity, Sita prays to Mother Earth and disappears as she is taken into her bosom on a golden throne. Sita is worshipped as a goddess, and revered as the ultimate symbol of an ideal woman who is pure, chaste, devoted to her god-like husband and silently bears the problems of life. This power of forbearance is regarded as a spiritual quality. Rama is once again grief stricken. He decides that the time had come for him to leave his mortal coil. He enters the sacred river Saryu near Ayodhya. It is said that he was absorbed into Vishnu, the Supreme God whose Incarnation he was.

Some Notes

No reading of the Ramayana is complete without a description of its central character. There are various

---

* The Ashvamedha is a sacrifice where a horse is sent to various kingdoms. If it is stopped anywhere, there is a war between the king of that region and the performer of the *yajna*.

descriptions of Rama throughout the epic. He was handsome and strong. He is dark complexioned. He was also *ajana bahu*, or one with long arms that reach up to the knees. He is brave, and the greatest of warriors. He is an affectionate and ideal son, husband, brother, father and friend. He always follows the *dharma*. He protects the good, the sages and the weak. He is always victorious. He is respectful of elders, and follows the ancient traditions, but also adheres to *satya*, the truth. He is considered to be an ideal man, or rather an incarnation of Vishnu, who shows us how an ideal man should conduct himself. Rama demonstrates the ideal of *dharma* and proper conduct.

Some parts of the Ramayana like the Aditya Hridayam, or the 'Sun (in the) Heart' are considered more sacred and are recited by some of the more devout Hindus. It has a philosophical aspect as well. There are some associated texts that were written much later. One such text is the Yoga Vasishtha, a highly philosophical text where Vasishtha teaches the young prince Rama. It is based on Vedanta. Rama wants to renounce the world seeing that it is impermanent. The sages are alarmed as they know that Rama is destined to perform many glorious deeds. Therefore, Vasishtha convinces the young prince that the same divinity can be found everywhere—in the world as well as in the forest. Rama reflects upon this and accepts the truth of this teaching. The text is regarded as a major philosophical work. Another text is the Adhyatma

Ramayana which also links the epic to the teachings of Vedanta.

Beginning from the medieval period, the Ramayana has been translated into various Indian languages. Ramayana storytelling or *path* is performed even today by trained storytellers and is heard by many people. In one version it is called the *akhand Ramayan path* where the verses are recited without a break, usually over several days. The modern digital age has slowly replaced this as a wealth of material is available online. The Ramayana is rarely read by people in the original Sanskrit. It is read in the local languages and heard in childhood from the elders. Festivals to celebrate various events in the life of Rama are held every year where stories about Rama's life are shared or depicted in drama, song and dance. The story of Rama has inspired saints and sages down the ages to compose several well-known songs that are sung even today. In some religious institutions, *Rama nama* or songs about Rama are sung regularly. *Rama nama* has a sacred meaning as it is regarded as a *mantra*, and repeating it said to lead to *moksha* or liberation. One fairly common religious practice is to write the name of Rama one crore (ten million) times. The Ramayana is very much a part of Indian religion and culture. Even in other countries such as Indonesia, a very popular Ramayana ballet is performed. It is part of the syncretic culture of a predominantly Muslim country. Many of the kings in Thailand named 'Rama'.

The Mahabharata

The Mahabharata is a later epic composed by Veda Vyasa. It contains around 74,000 verses and is more than three times the length of the Ramayana. Some versions of the epic contain around 100,000 verses.[*] Like the Ramayana, some regard only one part of the text as original, and say that there were later additions. It is a large complex epic with many stories and several characters. It does not revolve around any one central figure but has many heroic characters. Among them, the role of Krishna, an incarnation of Vishnu, is of primary importance.

The text is divided into eighteen sections or *parvas*. The epic does not run in a simple linear manner. There are several digressions, and stories about various events and kingdoms. Stories from more ancient times, myths, and legends are interwoven into the main story. It begins even before the central characters are born. Santanu, the King of the Lunar Dynasty fell in love with the beautiful Satyavati, the daughter of a chieftain of fishermen. The marriage is arranged but on the condition that Satyavati's sons would become kings. However, Santanu already had a son, Bhishma through a previous marriage with Ganga, the river goddess. Satyavati and her father then say that

---

[*] The Ramayana and the Mahabharata are sometimes compared to the Greek epics Iliad and Odyssey. The Mahabharata is about three times the combined length of the two great Greek epics.

in future Bhishma's children would claim the kingdom. Bhishma takes a vow that he would forsake the kingdom in favour of Satyavati's sons and that he would not marry and remain celibate. This vow is used in common language even today as Bhishma's pratigya or vow. It refers to any terrible vow undertaken by an individual.

Satyavati has two children, Chitrangada and Vichitravirya. To arrange for their marriage, their elder half-brother Bhishma attends the *swayamvara* (ceremony where princesses choose their husbands). He abducts Amba and brings her home as a bride for Vichitravirya. However, Amba confesses that she is already in love with another prince and therefore cannot marry Vichitravirya. Bhishma agrees and sends her back, after which Amba's two sisters, Ambika and Ambalika—who had also been abducted—are married to the two brothers. However, both the brothers die without any sons. Satyavati is worried about the lineage. As per the accepted practice of those times, she asks her son Bhishma to father sons through his brothers' widows. But, Bhishma refuses as he has taken a vow of celibacy. Satyavati then reveals that she had another son, none other than the great sage Veda Vyasa, born of the sage Parasara. She sends word and asks Vyasa to sire sons. Dhritarashtra and Pandu are born to the two sisters, and one more son, Vidura through a servant maid.

Dhritarashtra, the elder was born blind. So, his younger brother Pandu ruled instead. The understanding was that Dhritarashtra's eldest son would later become king. Dhritarashtra marries Gandhari, from the kingdom of Gandhar. This refers to modern Kandahar in Afghanistan. In deference to her husband, Gandhari voluntarily wears a blindfold. They have a hundred sons known as the Kauravas. The eldest was Duryodhana. Pandu had two wives, Kunti and Madri. Pandu was cursed to die if he entered into a union with a woman. Fortunately, Kunti had received a boon that she could give birth to sons by invoking the gods. While testing out this boon before marriage, she had given birth to Karna through the Sun God Surya. As an unwed mother she is forced to abandon him. Karna is brought up by a charioteer and his wife. After marriage to Pandu, Kunti gives birth to Yudhishthira or Dharmaraja, son of Yama, the God of Dharma, Bhima the son of Vayu, the God of wind and strength, and Arjuna the son of Indra, the King of the Gods. Madri invokes the boon from Kunti and gives birth to the twins Nakula and Sahadeva, born of the Asvins. The five sons are known as the Pandavas. Later, Pandu succumbs to the charms of Madri and dies. Madri accepts responsibility for her husband's death and immolates herself. Kunti becomes the mother for all of them.

The sons of Pandu called Pandavas and those of Dhritarashtra called the Kauravas are the principal characters in the Mahabharata. The Mahabharata describes the childhood of the Pandavas and the Kauravas. They were taught by Dronacharya, Kripacharya, Bhishma and other elders. They became skilled in the art of warfare. Yudhishthira the eldest, is respected for his adherence to truth and *dharma* and for his even, calm temperament. Bhima, the son of the wind God and of strength was renowned for his physical strength, in wrestling and in the art of cooking. Arjuna is renowned for his skill in archery. Nakula is skilled in swordsmanship and Ayurveda (medicine). He is also reputed for being very handsome. Sahadeva is skilled in swordsmanship, horsemanship and astrology. Since the Pandavas excel in everything, Duryodhana becomes jealous of them. He is also perhaps concerned that in the future, the Pandavas would lay claim to the kingdom. So, he plots and plans to finish them off using several tricks and ploys. In one such incident, they are invited to stay in a palace made of lac, an inflammable material. Duryodhana's plan was to set fire to the palace at night. However, the Pandavas get to know about it and escape.

Soon after, Draupadi becomes the wife of all five brothers. This is another well-known incident in the Mahabharata. Drupada, the father of Draupadi held a *swayamvara* to choose a husband for his daughter. The Pandavas were escaping from the palace of lac, and were incognito. But they decide to attend the ceremony as the king was giving away gifts to common people. The challenge was to hit a spinning fish on top with a special bow while looking only at its reflection in the water below. The epic describes various brave and handsome Princes who try their hand at it. Some could not even lift the bow. Karna, the great warrior did not win her hand. When everyone fails, Arjuna steps forward and shoots five arrows unerringly on target. Draupadi becomes his wife. On returning home, they tell their mother Kunti that they have brought some bhiksha or alms. Without looking she tells them that the brothers should share it among themselves. Draupadi thus becomes the wife of all five brothers. It is interesting to note that one of her names was Krishna, referring to her dark complexion. Draupadi was also one of the most beautiful of women.

The brothers come out into the open and return. Duryodhana pretends to be happy to see them. Dhritarashtra is concerned about the animosity between the cousins and gives them a large barren territory to rule. Yudhishthira is crowned as prince. He is very popular with the people and makes the kingdom prosperous. Duryodhana, who is also a prince, becomes even more jealous and insecure. In a dramatic confession to his maternal uncle, Sakuni, he says that seeing the fortune of the Pandavas, he felt jealous and was burning; that he would take poison and kill himself. Sakuni hatches a plan to get rid of the Pandavas. He knows that Yudhishthira was fond of a game of dice but was not good at it, while he, Sakuni, was an expert and would easily defeat him.

They persuade the blind king Dhritarashtra to invite the Pandavas for a game of dice. Duryodhana is forced to confess his jealously to his father. The King is not interested but is finally persuaded when Duryodhana threatens to kill himself otherwise.

As a respected elder, Dhitrarashtra's invitation is accepted by Yudhishthira. Sakuni is an expert in the game and plays on behalf of Duryodhana and wins all the games. Yudhishthira loses everything including his kingdom. He is tricked into playing one last round where he can win back everything if he stakes his wife Draupadi. He again loses.

Then follows a very dramatic episode in the Mahabharata which is a turning point and in many ways defines the rest of the epic. In great glee, Duryodhana asks that Draupadi be presented in the hall. She first asks the messenger who goes to fetch her 'what sort of a man or king would wager his wife?' and to go back to the hall and ask Yudhishthira, 'Did he wager himself first or wager me first?' When Yudhishthira sends word that she should come into the hall, she complies.

Dushasana, one of the hundred Kaurava brothers, drags Draupadi by her hair into the open assembly. When Draupadi repeats her questions, Duryodhana declares that the other Pandavas should say whether they accept Yudhishthira as their leader. They all say they do. Then the argument goes, that if he could wager them after losing himself, he could do the same for Draupadi. It is interesting to note that Draupadi never entreats her husbands to protect her. Draupadi beseeches the elders present. Bhishma, who is like a grandfather to the Pandavas and Kauravas says 'Subtle are the ways of *Dharma*. It is difficult to say what is right and what is wrong.' The question of whether a slave can wager his wife remains unresolved. The brothers are asked to strip off their garments as befits slaves. They remove their upper garments. Dushasana, grabs Draupadi's cloth and attempts wants to disrobe her. Everyone is shocked but silent. Only one of the Kaurava brothers, Vikarna protests against the insult of their sister-in-law Draupadi, as does a half-brother Yuyutsu but he is overruled. Vidura, a half-brother of the blind king Dhritarashtra also protests but is ignored.

Bhima is outraged and wants to kill the Kauravas. But Yudhishthira restrains both him and Arjuna. Duryodhana insultingly taps his thighs and asks Draupadi to sit on them. Karna calls Draupadi a whore for having five husbands against the Kshatriya *dharma*, and says the hundred brothers of the Kauravas can now be her husbands.

It was then that Arjuna takes a vow to kill Karna for insulting Draupadi. Bhima takes a vow to kill Duryodhana by smiting him in his thighs and loins and for insulting Draupadi. He also vows to drink the blood of Dushasana. All this came to pass more than thirteen years later during the epic war.

The lone and helpless Draupadi had no one to turn to. In an assembly of kings and wise men, there was no one to protect her as Dushasana begins disrobing her. She then prays to Krishna, the Incarnate God who is not physically present at the assembly. He then intervenes and the cloth keeps getting longer and longer and Dushasana is unable to succeed.

Dhritarashtra is alarmed by the turn of events and foresees disaster in the long run. He restores the wealth and freedom of his nephews, the Pandavas. As they return, Dhritarashtra is persuaded to invite them to a game of dice once again. In the second game, Yudhishthira once again loses. This time, however, they are banished into exile for twelve years and have to live a year more incognito. If they are discovered, then they have to go back into exile for another twelve years.

The Pandavas then leave for the forests. The epic describes various events during this period. One such famous episode is based on the *Yaksha Prasnas* or the questions of the (invisible) demigod. The brothers are exhausted and thirsty. The youngest, Sahadeva is sent to fetch water. He finds a beautiful lake.* Just as he is about to drink, the Yaksha's voice is heard and he hears that he must first answer his questions, failing which he will fall down dead. Sahadeva ignores the voice but almost immediately falls down as if

---

* Locals claim that Deoriyal Tal is the lake, which is near Ukhimath in Uttarakhand.

dead. When Sahadeva does not return, the next brother is sent in search of him. One by one, however, all the brothers fall down until only Yudhishthira is left. He also finds the lake and his brothers lying around. He however agrees to answer the questions which he does very well and his brothers are restored to life. The *Yaksha Prasnas* are deep, philosophical questions which elicit equally insightful answers. In response to the question of who is man's best friend, Yudhishthira answers that a loving wife is man's best friend. He also says that knowledge is the best possession, health the best gain and contentment the best happiness. Brahmins are distinguished by right conduct rather than their knowledge of the Vedas. One of the most astonishing things is that we know everyone dies but think that we will not die. The Yaksha reveals himself as Yama, the God of *dharma* and Death, the father of Yudhishthira. He is pleased with Yudhishthira's answers and restores his brothers to life.

After the twelve years, the Pandavas take employment with King Virata of the Matsya Kingdom for the '*agyatavasa*', the period of one year when they had to remain incognito. Yudhishthira became a minister, Bhima became a cook for the king, and Arjuna, disguised as a eunuch named Brihannala, taught dance and music to the king's daughter.* Nakula looks after the horses and

---

* Arjuna once went to heaven and repulsed the amorous advances of Urvashi, the most beautiful of the heavenly apsaras or damsels. She

Sahadev, the cows. Draupadi becomes a maid to the queen. There are several interesting stories from this period. In one such incident, the queen's brother, Kichaka is attracted to Draupadi. She warns him to stay away as her Gandharva husbands would kill him. This eventually come to pass when, by means of a ploy, Kichaka is lured by Draupadi to a location where Bhima (still in disguise) challenges him to a fight and kills him. The ever-present danger of discovery makes this sub-plot more interesting and thrilling.

Duryodhana suspects that the Pandavas are in disguise in the Matsya Kingdom. He sends his army there. They attack from various sides. Other than Arjuna, the other brothers help the king in this fight. However, when there is one more attack, the young prince persuades his mother to allow him to go and fight assisted by Brihannala. The period of *agyatavasa* was to end after sunset.* The battle is somehow averted for the day. The following day, Arjuna reveals his identity, twangs his divine bow Gandiva and

---

had a relationship with one of Arjuna's ancestors in the distant past and so he addresses her as Mother. Urvashi is insulted and curses him that he will become a eunuch. Indra, the father of Arjuna and the King of the Gods, requests Urvashi to soften her curse and so Arjuna's condition is reduced to one year. This is one of the typical digressions in the Mahabharata where several incidents are traced back to yet another more ancient story.

* The rules of war stipulated that there would be no fighting after sunset.

single handedly defeats the army the next day. Later in gratitude, the King gives his daughter Uttara in marriage to Arjuna's son Abhimanyu.

By this time, Duryodhana is even more determined that he will not give even an inch of his kingdom to the Pandavas. However, his attempt to prove that they had been discovered before their *agyatavasa* had come to an end fails. After some negotiations, the Pandavas agree to accept five villages as their territory. Duryodhana famously replies that he would not give so much land as could be found on a pin head.

War seems imminent. Several attempts are made to avert it. Krishna participates in several of these efforts. Once it becomes clear that war is inevitable, preparations begin on both sides. Most of the kings support the established ruler Duryodhana, but some supported the Pandavas. Krishna is related to both Arjuna and Duryodhana who go to meet him. He offers his army to one side, and says he alone would join the other side, but declares that he will not fight. Duryodhana chooses the army and Arjuna, the great friend and devotee chooses Krishna. All the elders, including Bhima, Drona and Kripa, fight for the Kauravas. Though highly revered and wise, they are compelled to do so by their *dharma* since they had enjoyed the patronage of Duryodhana and his father.

The epic describes in dramatic fashion the heroes, warriors, armies and weapons on display. Many of the weapons are of divine origin. In the midst of this battlefield, just as the war is about to begin, the Bhagavad Gita is taught by Krishna to Arjuna. This has been briefly discussed in an earlier chapter. The highest spiritual teachings are given for us when we are in the midst of the world, faced with challenges.

An eighteen-day war ensues. In one well-known incident, Abhimanyu, Arjuna's son, is killed. The young Abhimanyu had learnt from the womb of his mother Subhadra, sister of Krishna, one of the secrets of war—how to penetrate a battle formation called the Chakravyuha. But he did not learn how to break out of it. A mere lad of sixteen, he is lured into the Chakravyuha. He fights valiantly and destroys many of the enemy soldiers but is eventually killed. Arjuna is paralyzed by grief.* Abhimanyu's wife, Uttara, who was pregnant at the time of his death, gives birth to Parikshit who continues the Lunar dynasty. Later, Parikshit receives the Bhagavatam, one of the most popular Puranas, from the sage Suka, son of Veda Vyasa. Bhima's son, Ghatotkacha† fights valiantly for the Pandavas but is

---

* A few days earlier, Arjuna heard Krishna expounding the Bhagavad Gita saying that the soul is immortal, that the body is discarded as a worn-out garment. So there is no need to grieve. But the human side of Arjuna prevails and he grieves. Arjuna has not yet become an established sage, but is human like all of us.

† Ghatotkacha was the son of Bhima and Hidimba, an *asura* or *rakshasa* woman, and possessed magical powers.

killed by Karna. Karna is forced to use one of his divine weapons to kill Ghatotkacha, who was causing immense damage to the Kaurava armies. As a result, Karna has one less weapon for his future battle with Arjuna.

One after the other, the great generals Bhishma, Drona and Karna take command and one after the other, they are killed. The strategies used to defeat them are given. Bhishma is almost invincible and has a boon that he would die by his own wish. When Krishna finds that Bhishma cannot be defeated, he takes up weapons and rushes towards Bhishma, apparently forgetting his vow of not taking up arms. Bhishma is pleased that he would die at the hands of the Lord. However, Arjuna reminds Krishna of his vow, who then comes back without attacking Bhishma. In an earlier incident Bhishma had said that he would make Krishna take up arms and Krishna, ever ready to please his devotees, does so. Sikhandi, a eunuch, is roped in to help Arjuna. She is none other than Amba who had been abducted by Bhishma to marry her off to his two half-brothers. She vows to take revenge and is reborn as Sikhandi. When Bhishma sees Sikhandi he recognizes her as Amba and refuses to fight a woman. Finally, Arjuna pierces Bhishma with his arrows and he lies down on the battlefield. As foretold, he gives up his life after nearly three months waiting for the auspicious time when the Sun would move northwards. During this period, he teaches Yudhishthira about the *dharma* of a king and gives several wise instructions.

Drona, the next commander, is also invincible. However, his weakness is his son, Aswathama, a fact which is known to the Pandavas. Yudhishthira is persuaded to announce that Aswathama is dead (and in a whisper he adds 'the elephant' mentioning an elephant of the same name). Since he is known for his adherence to truth, Drona believes that it is his son who was killed. Losing all motivation, Drona lays down his arms and is killed. For telling this lie, the chariot of Yudhishthira which always hovered a few inches above the ground, sinks and touches the earth. In accordance with the rules of war, fighting stops at sunset. However, Aswathama, who is angered by the deceitful way his father Drona was killed, breaks the law and kills all the surviving sons of the Pandavas when they were sleeping. Aswathama was said to be *chiranjivi* or immortal. He was the son of the *guru*, Dronacharya who was also *guru* to Arjuna and the Pandavas.

In another famous incident, Arjuna vows to kill Jayadratha before the sun sets the following day or immolate himself. Jayadratha had abducted Draupadi when they were in exile in the forest. He had been defeated and forgiven by Draupadi herself as he was related to them through his wife who was the sister of the Kauravas. However, Jayadratha deceitfully kills Arjuna's son, Abhimanyu and so Arjuna vows to kill him. The next day as the sun is about to set, Krishna covers the sun, thereby creating an illusion of sunset. Although there was a massive army separating the two camps, an overjoyed Jayadratha makes the mistake of showing himself. Krishna then uncovers the sun and Arjuna kills Jayadratha.

Karna is the next general. He is the greatest of warriors, the equal of Arjuna. He is famous for his charity. He also has divine weapons and protection that he obtained by means of great austerity or *tapas*. However, even before the war, Indra, the King of the Gods, had asked for his earrings which protected Karna and had taken them away. Karna was also forced to use one of his weapons to kill Ghatotkacha.

Earlier, Karna had tried to obtain the divine weapon, Brahmastra from his *guru* Dronacharya. However, he refused to teach him as he had already taught Arjuna, his favourite disciple. Karna subsequently obtained the weapon from Parasurama. Since Parasurama only taught Brahmins, Karna had pretended to be one. When Parasurama discovered that Karna was a Kshatriya, he cursed him, declaring that he would forget the *mantra* to invoke the Brahmastra precisely when it was most crucial.

During the battle between Arjuna and Karna, the wheel of Karna's chariot gets stuck in the mud. Karna gets down to haul it up and reminds Arjuna of the rules of war which do not allow attacking the enemy at such a time. Krishna incites Arjuna, reminding him how his son Abhimanyu had been deceitfully killed by Karna and how Draupadi had been insulted. Due to Parasurama's curse,

Karna forgets the *mantra* to protect himself. Arjuna slays him and fulfils the vow he had taken when Draupadi was being humiliated.

It is interesting to note that all the three generals who commanded the Kaurava armies—Bhishma, Drona and Karna—were invincible. However, all are defeated either by strategy or by a turn of fate. Krishna, though present as a charioteer, never uses any of his divine powers to defeat them.

Duryodhana and Dushasana are both killed by Bhima. As promised, Bhima drinks Dushasana's blood and smears Draupadi's hair with it to avenge her insult. Duryodhana fights a duel with Bhima. During this duel, Krishna reminds Bhima of the way in which Duryodhana had insulted Draupadi by slapping his thighs. Bhima is enraged and strikes Duryodhana on the thighs and loins, thus bringing him down. Duryodhana complains that he has been beaten by breaking the rules as striking below the waist was forbidden. As he lies dying, he boasts that he had enjoyed his kingdom whereas the Pandavas had spent most of their lives in the forest and had lost all their sons. What would they enjoy? Duryodhana also tells Krishna in an oft-quoted verse that he knew what was right, but did not do it, and he knew what was wrong but still did it. When Duryodhana utters these lines, he seems to speak for all of us. He is not depicted as an entirely evil person. His only flaws were envy and jealousy. He was a good king, loyal to his friends, brave, the best warrior to ever wield a mace and willing to face death. When he lay dying even the gods showered flowers on him.

After the war, Yudhishthira rules as king and performs the Ashvamedha *yajna* just as Rama had done long ago. During the *yajna*, a half-golden mongoose is found rolling on the flour that had been spilt on the floor. When questioned, the mongoose narrates a story. A poor householder, who had been starving, was visited by a guest who came asking for food. Following the *dharma* of the householder, his family cheerfully gave away all their food to the guest. But they fall dead due to starvation. The mongoose chanced upon the flour spilt on the floor, and as he rolled on it, half his body turned golden. Ever since he had been looking for an equally great sacrifice to make his whole body golden. The moral of the story is that the great Ashvamedha sacrifice performed by Emperor Yudhishthira did not match the sacrifice of the poor householder.

At the end of the Mahabharata, the Pandavas leave for heaven.* One by one, Draupadi and all the Pandavas, except Yudhishthira, fall dead on their way. The epic describes some small flaw either in the character of

---

* Swargarohini, a well-known Himalayan peak in Uttarakhand, is said to be the mountain climbed by the Pandavas climbed on their way to heaven.

Draupadi and each of the four brothers or some wrong action they committed. Yudhishthira alone is able to reach the gates of heaven. However, there is a black dog that accompanies him throughout. Yudhishthira insists that the dog be admitted to heaven. When that is denied, he too refuses to enter. Then it is revealed that the dog is actually his father Yama, the God of Dharma and Death, who had accompanied his son to test him. Yudhishthira passes the final test and goes to heaven.

Some Notes

This brief outline offers only a glimpse into the wealth of stories and details in the epic. It has a discussion on the four goals of life, namely *dharma* or right conduct, *artha* or material prosperity, *kama* or fulfilment of desires, and *moksha* or final liberation. It also contains several love stories about Shakuntala and Dushyanta, (this was also written as a classic drama centuries later in Sanskrit by Kalidasa), Nala and Damayanti, the story of Savitri and Satyavan where the chaste wife Savitri rescues her husband Satyavan from death, and the story of Kacha and Devyani. These stories are narrated during the period of the Pandavas' exile in the forest.

The Mahabharata is a Great Epic with descriptions of heroes, gods, armies and weapons. It narrates several events, each of which is an interesting story in its own right. It always raises questions of *dharma* and about what is right and what is wrong. Sometimes it even says that this is difficult to decide. The defeated Kauravas, including Bhishma, Drona, Karna and even Duryodhana, are not painted in black and white. All of them are defeated using various stratagems.

Karna, in particular, is portrayed as a great warrior, equal to Arjuna in archery, loyal to his friend, Duryodhana who bestowed a kingdom on him, and the most generous of men who was unsurpassed in charity. He was wronged because his unwed mother abandoned him. He even promised her that other than Arjuna, he would not kill any of his brothers. He fulfilled his promise when he defeats Yudhishthira, Nakula and Sahadeva in the epic war, but spares their lives. In short, the characters and events are more complex and there is a lot of discussion on what is *dharma*.

The entire range of human desires, motivations and emotions are poetically depicted. The epic describes Duryodhana's jealousy, Dhritarashtra's blind affection for his son, Karna's unparalleled charity, Yudhishthira's adherence to truth, Arjuna's skill as a warrior and his human weaknesses, Bhishma's wisdom as well as the traits and characteristics of several others. There are dramatic situations throwing up questions on ethics, *dharma*, rules of war, and nuanced discussions about what is right. The Mahabharata has a universal aspect because its lessons apply to the human condition even today. Its stories and events continue to be read and narrated. In the midst of all this, Krishna himself becomes the exemplar of the detached actor, the divine actor in the world, preaching the Bhagavad Gita in the middle of the battlefield. According to one tradition, the Mahabharata is said to be the fifth Veda.

11

THE GREAT PHILOSOPHIES

After the epic period, several commentaries were written
on various texts. This period spanned several centuries.
The Puranas and Agama Sastras, were also compiled
over centuries, From the 7th century BCE, several schools
of philosophy emerged. The principal ones were based
on the Upanishads and the Brahma Sutras. The well-
known philosophies that are available today are the
Advaita, Visishtadvaita and Dvaita. In addition, there are
the Shudhadvaita and Dvaitadvaita, variations of which
are known as the Bhedabheda Vada and the Achintya
Bhedabheda. In addition, the Ajata vada, Drishti Shrishti
vada and Shristhi Drishti vada philosophies emerged which
are different ways of understanding the reality, the world,
the individual and the relationships between them.

The ideas in these philosophies were present in some
form even in earlier times. We find references to the ideas
expounded in these philosophies not only in earlier texts,
but also in other religions such as Jainism and Buddhism.

However, Jainism and Buddhism did not exist at that time, and these ideas were later developed into full-fledged philosophies. The same is true of the Vedantic philosophies. The authors of these philosophies in a sense did not create anything new, but put earlier ideas into a systematic form. All the Vedantic philosophies are based on the Upanishads and the Brahma Sutras.

If these later philosophies are based are the same texts, then why are they different? Scholars give various reasons. The aphorisms in the Brahma Sutras are very condensed and terse. They may have been aids to memory using which long discussions between teacher and student took place. Several writings known as the *vakyas*, *vrittis*, *karikas* and *bhashyas*, each with an explanation more elaborate than the previous one, were written. These texts are open to interpretation. Some verses change their meaning if the pauses are changed slightly. There are two opposing points of view presented by the *Purvapaksha*, which gives one side of the argument and the *Siddhanta*, which establishes the truth. There is no clear demarcation between the two, leaving it to the interpreter to decide which is the truth. Some statements in the Brahma Sutras do not give the reference of the Upanishad from which they are taken. The commentator is free to select and quote what he believes are the relevant Upanishadic verses. Badarayana is also often silent about his own point of view, and merely states the *sutras* and summarizes different points of view.

The great commentators and their philosophies, however, agree on some basic issues. One is the supremacy of the Vedanta and refuting non-Vedic ideas. Recall that non-Vedic ideas from what later developed into Jainism and Buddhism predated these religions and existed in an earlier form when the Brahma Sutras were composed. Such ideas are clearly refuted in the Brahma Sutras and by all later commentators. They also agree that Brahman exists, that knowledge of it gives liberation, and that liberation is the goal of life. They also agree on the importance of imbibing the real essence of the scriptures and not on mere intellectual understanding. However, commentators disagree about the precise nature of Brahman, the means to attain it, the nature of the human soul, the world and their relation to Brahman.

The words 'real' and 'unreal' are used repeatedly. Here it means something different. That which is unchanging and eternal is Real. That which changes or disappears or is destroyed is not real.

The unreal may *seem* real, but that is only a temporary illusion. A cloud that dissipates or showers rain is not real according to Vedanta. Dreams are not real though they seem to be so at the time of dreaming. Advaita says the world is unreal because it is always changing and perhaps will eventually be destroyed. Visishtadvaita and Dvaita say the world is real and eternal. Visishtadvaita says the world is an attribute of the unchanging, eternal Brahman. Dvaita says the world is separate and different from Brahman, and permanent, and hence is real.

Advaita

Advaita was the first of the three Great Philosophies. Its most significant proponent was Adi Sankara in the 8th century ce. However, as stated earlier, Advaitic ideas existed long before that. Gaudapada, the *guru* of Adi Sankara's *guru*, wrote the well-known Karika on the Mandukya Upanishad (on which Sankara wrote a *bhashya* or commentary) also developed Advaitic ideas. Advaita has been extensively written about and commented on in various languages. The essential idea is from the word '*advaita*' itself which means 'non-dual'. Thus, Brahman is the One all-pervading Reality. Therefore, it cannot be described in relation to anything else. Since it is infinite, it is *nirguna,* attribute-less and *nirakara*, formless. Even attributes like omnipotence are constructs of the mind whereas Brahman is beyond that. It is also formless since forms would limit it. Since there is no duality, Brahman, the universe and the *jivas* or individuals are also Brahman.

Brahman is *Sat-Chit-Ananda* (existence–knowledge–bliss). These are not attributes but the very essence of Brahman—the closest we can come to describing it. Thus, Brahman 'Is' the One Being without a second. It is Consciousness, that leads to knowledge, and full of *ananda* or bliss.

However, what about the world and the living beings? Sankara uses the idea of '*maya*' to explain this. The similes of the serpent and the rope, or of a mirage in a desert are repeatedly invoked. In a semi-dark room, a rope is mistaken for a serpent causing fear. However, the light of knowledge reveals that it is merely a rope. A visit to the actual location of the mirage shows that there is no water. Knowledge, therefore, is sufficient to remove ignorance. In the same way, the world we see around us is like a mirage and has no real existence. A famous quote of Sankara is '*Brahma satya, jagat mithya*', that is, Brahman is real the world is false.

In Advaita, Brahman in its manifest aspect Ishwara or God, is also *maya*. This is the highest conception that an individual can have of the *nirguna* and *nirakara* Brahman. It is both the efficient and the material cause of the universe. Unlike a potter who is only the efficient cause of a pot but is not the clay, Brahman as Ishwara is the universe, much like a spider weaves a web from its own body. Brahman pervades the universe and all living beings.

The Upanishadic *mahavakyas* '*Aham Brahmasmi*' or 'I am Brahman', and '*Ayam Atma Brahma*' or 'this Self or Atman is Brahman' are quoted to establish that the individual is also Brahman. Some of the Upanishadic statements use the term '*advaita*', for instance *sivo-advaita*, 'peaceful and non-dual' from the Mandukya Upanishad, and *ekam eva advitiyam*, 'there is only One without a second' from the Maitreya Upanishad. The Self or Atman is not merely a part of Brahman, as there are no parts and there cannot be two.

Once the knowledge of Brahman is obtained, the goal of human life is attained. The individual is also freed from rebirth since desires—which are the cause of rebirth—cease upon gaining knowledge. This can be attained in the here and now rather than after death. The actions, enjoyments and suffering of a living *jnani* or knower of Brahman are only from the point of view of the onlooker. For the *jnani* it is like a dream.

Advaita also says that the theory of *maya* is only from the relative point of view of the individual. For the *jnani* or sage established in the Truth, there is no *maya*. Just like someone who knows that the serpent is actually a rope, the *jnani* is never again deluded. The false perception of the snake is from the relative perspective. There was never any snake in the first place.

The methods used by Sankara to establish Advaita are also worth noting. He uses reason, simile, the Brahma Sutras and the Upanishads to establish his principles. He does not claim any mystical experience to establish Advaita although by common consent he was a *jnani* himself.

Notes

The Advaita generally appeals to spiritual seekers who have a rational bent of mind or those who are from non-Hindu backgrounds. The *dasanami* sects of monks or *sannyasins* are Advaitins. Traditionally, Haridwar, Rishikesh and Varanasi are centres of Advaitic philosophy.

Advaita emphasizes knowledge as the means to liberation, although it also endorses devotion or *bhakti*. However, *bhakti* is defined as a longing for liberation, freedom, peace and joy, which is a means and not an end.

There are several other texts on Advaita. Some of the scriptures like the Avadhuta Gita implicitly expound Advaita. Since God or Ishwara is also part of *maya* in Advaita, it does not really accept the concept of the *avatar* or Incarnation of God.

Traditionally, Siva is associated with Advaita. Although independent Saivite philosophies developed, Sankara says in Nirvana Satakam '*Chidananda roopa, Sivoham, Sivoham*' as a refrain at the end of every stanza. Siva here refers to Brahman.

Other notable writers on Advaita from earlier times include Gaudapada who predates Sankara, Suresvara, Vidyaranya and Sadananda. Sankara himself wrote several texts including commentaries on the Principal Upanishads, the Bhagavad Gita, as well as Vivekachudamani, Atmabodha, Upadesa Sahasri, Aparokshanubhuti, Drig Drishya Vivekam, Tatytva Bodha and several poems and even devotional hymns. Some scholars say that others may have written some of these texts.

Visishtadvaita

Historically, the Visishtadvaita came after the Advaita in the late 11th and early 12th century CE. It means qualified non-dualism. Its greatest proponent was Sri Ramanujacharya, who wrote the well-known Sri Bhashya or commentary on the Brahma Sutras. He also referred to a commentary on the Brahma Sutras called the Bodhayana which is lost today. He, like Sankara before him, refers to the Upanishads in his commentary.

Visishtadvaita says that Brahman is the Ultimate Reality and is identical with Narayana, a Personal God. It is not *nirguna* as described by the Advaita. It is *saguna* Brahman, with attributes. Brahman or *Narayana* is supreme and is qualified by the world and its living beings. '*Visishta*' means 'qualified by attributes'. The world is not a mirage but is real. It explicitly negates the theory of *maya* in Advaita. Matter is insentient or unconscious, yet real. The living beings are sentient and also real. Thus, Reality has three aspects—*para* Brahman or the Supreme Reality that is beyond; *chit* Brahman or the sentient living beings; and *achit* Brahman or insentient matter. All three are aspects of Brahman.

Narayana is the material and efficient creator of the world. He has several attributes and is omniscient, omnipotent, Lord of the Universe, worthy of worship, without a body. He is also the indweller in all sentient beings.

Upanishadic statements like '*satyam jnanam anantam Brahma*' are quoted to establish that Brahman is Truth, Knowledge and Infinity. According to Visishtadvaita, even the lack of attributes is an attribute. Something that is *nirguna* cannot be cognized; it is only through attributes that Brahman can be known.

The great *mahavakyas* in the Upanishads that are given an Advaitic interpretation by Sankara are explained differently by Visishtadvaita. Sarvam khalvidam brahma, or all is Brahman is true because *Para* Brahman, *chit* Brahman and *achit* Brahman are all part of the same Brahman. The phrase *Tat tvam asi* or 'That thou art' means the *jiva* is identical to Brahman in essence but is not Brahman itself.

Devotion or *bhakti* is the primary means of knowing God, although knowledge is also accepted as a secondary means. The individual souls are all identical and, in essence, the same as Narayana. Liberation comes after the soul is released from the body for those who have reached the goal of life. Liberation means entering *Vaikuntha*, the abode of God, and living in His presence in a state of everlasting bliss. There is no rebirth. Unlike Advaita, there is no jivanmukta, or liberation while in the body.

The concept of liberation in Visishtadvaita is different from Advaita where it comes from knowledge and complete removal of ignorance. The *jiva* knows it is one with Brahman and is liberated. In Visishtadvaita, liberation comes from supreme devotion, through the grace of God.

It is attained after death and takes the *jiva* to Vaikuntha where it enjoys eternal bliss but remains separate from Brahman.

Some Notes

This gives only a brief overview of the philosophy. Visishtadvaita gives many details about how to attain *bhakti*. It uses the terms *saranagati*, literally taking shelter under, and *prapatti* or surrender. Scholars differentiate between the two. *Saranagati* means taking refuge in God to obtain His grace. *Prapatti* means surrendering the ego to God, leaving everything in His hands. Some analogies may illustrate this. The baby monkey clings to the mother as it jumps around on trees and elsewhere. It takes refuge in the mother. It is *saranagati*. The kitten on the other hand lies in a corner and simply mews. The mother picks it up and does what it pleases with it. Similarly, the devotee who has attained prapatti accepts whatever God gives him. Visishtadvaita says that ultimately the ego has to be surrendered by prapatti. Otherwise, the grace of God obtained by surrender can lead to rewards that can further strengthen the ego.*

---

* Getting rid of the ego completely is a part of both Advaita and Buddhism. Knowledge is the means for achieving this as the ego is seen as unreal. In the path of devotion, the ego is surrendered to God. All these approaches lead to liberation or *nirvana*.

Worship, rituals and various means are prescribed for attaining *bhakti*. Visishtadvaita appeals to those who are inclined to devotion. It is also very difficult to imagine and strive after an attribute-less, formless Brahman as in Advaita. A real world, a real Personal God makes it much easier to cultivate such devotion. It is almost impossible for most individuals to accept that they are the same as Brahman. *Bhakti*, even in the Advaita, is said to be *Jnana Mata* or the Mother of Knowledge.

Ramanujacharya also used simple and clear means to establish the truth. *Pramana* or correct knowledge is obtained by three means. *Pratyaksha* or direct sensory knowledge, *anumana* or knowledge by inference and *sabda* or the word of the scriptures. Using these three the philosophy of Visishtadvaita is established. His first *guru* belonged to the Advaita tradition. Temperamentally opposed to it, the young Ramanuja did not accept his *guru*'s teachings and after several arguments, left to pursue his own path. Ramanuja went over to the pre-existing devotional and Vaishnava tradition which included the great Alwar saints, as well as earlier teachers.

The Upanishads have several statements. Some emphasize non-duality whereas others uphold plurality. Ramanujacharya argued that all of them should be taken into account and that qualified non-dualism alone could reconcile them. Sankara had earlier argued that the entire text must be taken as one, and the real purpose understood. From this standpoint, some of the statements in the Upanishads were expository and used analogies and symbols. They were not to be taken literally. Ramanuja disagreed and says it is not correct to decide what is to be accepted as it is and what is to be taken as illustration. Since there are statements showing that Brahman is the cause of the universe and the living beings, the threefold ontology of *Para* Brahman, *chit* Brahman and *achit* Brahman alone explains what the Upanishads meant.

Ramanujacharya also wrote many other sacred texts. The Sri Bhashya, the commentary on the Brahma Sutras, is the most well-known. This established the foundation of the Visishtadvaita philosophy. He wrote a *bhashya* on the Bhagavad Gita as well as the Vedarthasangraha, a treatise on the meaning of the Vedas. He is also credited with the composition of several other texts. In addition to Sanskrit, he also wrote several texts in Tamil. Ramanujacharya was preceded and followed by a number of Vaishnava writers, such as the Alwars, Nathamuni, Yamunacharya, who preceded him and Vedanta Desikar, Pillai Lokacharya and others, who succeeded him. As with the other philosophies, the ideas relating to Visishtadvaita were there long before Ramanujacharya. However, he is the major figure who expounded those ideas and established a sound philosophy based on devotion.

Though developed in south India, its influence reached far-away Bengal and was carried forward by Sri Chaitanya

Mahaprabhu centuries later, whose followers established another philosophy. Chaitanya travelled to the south of India out of respect for Ramanujacharya. Visishtadvaita also influenced the Ramanandis in north India, who also believe in Vishnu and the incarnations who alone can give liberation. Later differences may have developed, but Ramanujacharya was their earliest inspiration.

Dvaita

Dvaita came after both the Advaita and Visishtadvaita. The word literally means dual. It was first propounded by Sri Madhvacharya, also known as Ananda Tirtha and *Purnapragna* (one with complete Consciousness or knowledge) in the 13th century. Madhvacharya uses the Vedas, Upanishads and the Brahma Sutras to establish the philosophy of Dvaita. It is also known as *bheda vada, tattva vada* and as *Purnabrahma vada*.

Dvaita also accepts the Vedas and Upanishads. It bases its philosophy on the Brahma Sutras and the Upanishads. According to Dvaita, Brahman is the Supreme Reality and is identified with Narayana or Vishnu. It is the experience of everyone that God is different from a human being, a premise which the Dvaita says is true. We also say that living beings and matter are different. This is also accepted as true. There are three fundamental realities: God, living beings and matter. They are all different from each other.

Brahman as Vishnu is the *svatantra tattva* or independent reality. He is omnipotent, eternal, omniscient and compassionate. Brahman is identified with Vishnu and Madhvacharya says '*brahmaśabdaśca Viṣṇaveva*', meaning the word of the scripture refers to Vishnu alone. The world or universe and the living beings are *asvatantra tattva* or dependent reality. God is the ruler and controller of everything. All other gods and *devas* are subservient to Vishnu. To refute earlier philosophies, it says God could not have changed Himself into such an imperfect world. The individual souls are reflections of Brahman but not identical with it in any way. Evil, suffering and misery is not caused by God but by *jivas* who enjoy or suffer according to their deeds and *karma*.

Dvaita says that there are five eternal dualities. The first is between God and living beings, the second is between God and matter, the third is between living beings and matter. A fourth is between different individuals and the fifth is between different types of matter. These five dualities are eternal.

God is all-powerful and omniscient. He governs the universe and all living beings and is *Sat-Chit-Ananda*. He has a non-material body since He is different from matter. There are three types of souls. The first type is *mukti yogyas* or those fit for liberation who eventually achieve such liberation. This means understanding that we are eternally dependent on God, that we are but reflections of Him but not identical to Him. Knowing that we are dependent on Him is essential. God allows us to a degree of freedom which is determined by our *karma*. Ignorance is the root cause of misery, as other philosophies say. This can be removed by devotion, by right action and even by intuition. Devotion to God may be more important than any liberation. God shows us the way through several *avatars*. This category of people attain bliss but are separate from God. The level of bliss depends on their devotion. The second category are *nitya samsaris* who are born again and again. The third type is *tamo yogyas* who are condemned to eternal hell. This is the only philosophy in Hinduism that talks of eternal hell. All other philosophies say that everyone is ultimately liberated even if takes several births to do so.

Dvaita says that God gives free will to human beings but also controls them. Other philosophies do not give much importance to the question of whether there is an individual free will. They say that if our *karma* and desires based on the law of cause and effect lead to action, where is the free will? Dvaita, however, disagrees and says individuals do have some free will.

Some Notes

The Dvaita is a realist philosophy that accepts the normal everyday experience of everyone where individuals are different from each other and from matter, and where there are different types of matter. However, unlike atheists, it holds that there is a God. God is separate from both living beings and matter. It is the closest to the monotheistic religions of the world.

Dvaita also refutes other philosophies, particularly Advaita. It also refutes some aspects of Visishtadvaita. While Dvaita agrees that Narayana is identical with Brahman, and that both the *jivas* and the universe are different from it, Dvaita says that the *jivas* are not even in essence identical with Brahman, they are mere reflections at best. It also rejects qualified monism which holds that Brahman is qualified by the world and living beings. Dvaita says these three—Brahman, the world and living beings—are fundamentally different. It uses logic and scriptural authority in order to do so. There are three means of knowledge—*pratyaksha* or direct sensory experience, *anumana* or inference and *sabda* or the word of scripture. This is similar to the means of knowledge that Visishtadvaita uses. Unlike Advaita, Dvaita says that the knower and the known are independent realities. It is in essence opposed to Advaita.

Madhvacharya wrote around thirty-seven texts, including *bhashyas* or commentaries on the Principal Upanishads. It has influenced later schools of thought. One of the great saints of this schools is Raghavendra Swami. Scholars in this tradition include Jayatirtha, Vyasatirtha, Vadiraja Tirtha, Raghuttama Tirtha and Satyanatha Tirtha.

A Brief Summary

These three Great Philosophies are widely prevalent today. The following table provides a summary.

Philosophy	Advaita	Visishtadvaita	Dvaita
Basis	Advaita or non-dualism says that the formless, attribute-less Brahman is the only reality, the Absolute.	Visishtadvaita is Qualfied non-dualism where Brahman is qualified by the material universe and by living beings.	Brahman is equated with Vishnu and is said to be the highest reality. It is separate from the universe and from living beings.
God	Ishwara or God is the personal but formless aspect of Brahman. Ultimately Ishwara is also *maya* or illusion. Only the formless, attribute-less Brahman exists.	God is Narayana or Vishnu. He is the Immanent and the Transcendent Reality. He is the formless Creator and is immanent in the universe.	God is Narayana or Vishnu who is also formless. He is separate from matter and from living beings.
Universe	The Universe is *maya* or an illusion.	The universe is real but is an attribute of Brahman.	The universe is real and separate from Brahman.
Goal of life	Liberation from rebirth by the individual soul merging with Brahman.	Liberation from rebirth. Going to Vaikuntha or God's eternal abode and forever remaining there in a state of bliss.	Liberation. Going to God's eternal abode. Level of bliss depends upon the individual soul.
Who can get liberation	All living beings will ultimately achieve liberation.	All living beings will ultimately achieve liberation.	Only souls fit for liberation achieve it. Some souls are born again and again. The rest go to eternal hell.

Other Philosophies

Shudhadvaita and Bhedabheda, which are variations of the devotional aspect of philosophy, emerged later. Bhedabheda literally means different and non-different. This was elaborated by Nimbarka and later by Chaitanya as well. Brahman and its power of manifestation, *Sakti* are neither different from each other, nor identical. Analogies such as the heat and light from the sun as well as the gem and its lustre are used to illustrate this. It also says that mere reasoning cannot establish this. Shudhadvaita was first propounded by Vallabhacharya. According to this philosophy, the individual soul is identical to Brahman but only to a minuscule part of it. Krishna is the supreme goal of life. Like the Visishtadvaita and Dvaita, both these schools of philosophy are from the Bhakti tradition.

Advaita based on Knowledge also has some other doctrines. *Shrishti Drishti vada* says that the world was created and is therefore visible. This is a realist view that accepts the experience of the senses and the mind. *Drishti Shristi vada*, on the other hand, says that the mind creates the universe. Without an observer, there is nothing out there. It implies that the world is not real but is a projection of the mind. The world we experience in dreams becomes unreal on waking up. Similarly, the world we see disappears when we gain knowledge of Brahman. For those who do not accept this premise, the earlier *Shristi Drishti vada* is recommended. Advaita says that the world and all living beings and phenomena arise from *maya*, which is said to be *anirvachaniya* which means inexpressible. This is from the standpoint of the mind and what it experiences. Ajata vada goes beyond that and says there is no world, no creation, no bondage, no liberation. There is only One. Ajata literally means unborn.* It says nothing exists except the one reality. There is no birth or death, no projection or drawing in of the world, no *sadhaka* or seeker, no *mumukshu* or one seeking liberation, no *mukta* or liberated person, no bondage, no liberation. The one unity alone exists.' There is no *maya* either. Ajata vada is from the standpoint of the *jnani* and his experience. One analogy is that in bright sunlight, one cannot see a movie on a screen.'† Similarly, for the fully enlightened *jnani*, there is only the One and nothing else. *Maya* arises from the standpoint of the seeker who is not yet enlightened. Gaudapada refers to *ajata vada* in the Mandukya Karika. He predates Sankara and was his *guru's guru*. Some of Sankara's texts also have passages that are *ajata vada*. Various texts like the Ashtavakra, Ribhu and Avadhuta Gita, and some parts of the Yoga Vasishtha are also identical to *ajata vada*.

---

* This is similar to the Madhaymika philosophy of Buddhism which talks of non-origination. However, Ajata says that it is Brahman that is unborn while Madhyamika says it is *shunya* or nothingness.
† Conversations with Ramana Maharshi, March 1946.

Conclusions

It is worth noting that the originators of all these philosophies were not mere scholars but are widely considered spiritually enlightened. Then, if Truth is one, why are there so many philosophies?[1] This Reality or Truth is said to be beyond the mind and senses, but yet can be experienced. That experience is then sought to be conveyed in words, which are the domain of the mind and the senses. The same person who experiences these revelations interprets them and puts them into words. The minds of such illumined individuals are the instruments for propounding these philosophies. Some explain these differences on this basis. Others, however, add that even the revelation depends upon the seer. While the experiences are super-sensory and bring joy and peace, they are received according to the mind of the seer. Such subjectivity of interpretation might be another reason for the differences between the different schools.

However, despite differences, there are some common precepts as well. Surrendering the ego through devotion or eliminating it through knowledge both point to the need for getting rid of the ego which is a barrier to revelation. The necessity of keeping the mind calm, focused and free of negative emotions is also accepted by all of them. All the philosophies point to liberation, a state that provides permanent joy and peace.

On the positive side, the wide variety of philosophies allows each individual to accept the one that most appeals to him. All of them lead the seeker forward and show a way of making life more peaceful, joyful and meaningful. If there was only one philosophy, it would not appeal to people of widely different temperaments. Vivekananda says, 'The end seems, therefore, to be not destruction but a multiplication of sects until each individual is a sect unto himself.'[2] This recognizes the need for each individual to chart out and choose his or her own path. The Rig Veda says, '*ekam Sat, vipra bahuda vadanti*', Truth is One, sages call it by different names.

12

THE BHAKTI TRADITION

So far, the texts discussed were in Sanskrit. However, there are many other texts in regional languages. Perhaps the first was in ancient times, when Buddha preached in Pali, and exhorted his followers to spread the Dhamma or teaching everywhere in the language of the people. Sanskrit was not spoken by the majority of the people. Tamil literature, also from ancient times, had several religious texts. In the medieval period, saints and sages from every region of India disseminated their teachings in the local languages. This perhaps had more influence on the people than the Sanskrit texts.

It is impossible to give a detailed account of these texts. Some of the well-known teachings come from the entire length and breadth of the country. They included saints from all castes and communities as well as men and women. There was also an undercurrent of so-called lower-caste religious movements. Thus, there were *bauls* in Bengal, the Ramananda sampradiyis and Kabir panthis from north

India, the saints of Rajasthan, Gujarat and Maharashtra, the Alwars and Nayanars from Tamil Nadu and saints from other regions. Some well-known names include Chaitanya Mahaprabhu, Ramprasad and Kamalakanta from Bengal, Jayadev and the five saints or *Pancha Sakhas* Balarama Das, Jagannatha Das, Achyutananda Das, Yasobanta Das and Sisu Ananta Das from Odisha; Shankaradeva from Assam; Tulsidas, Surdas, Bilwamangal, Ramanand, Kabir, Haridas, Ravidass, Matsyendranath and Gorakhnath who wrote in the language of their regions which were a precursor to modern Hindi; Meerabai and Dadu from Rajasthan; Narsi Mehta from Gujarat; Jnaneswar, Tukaram, Namdev, Eknath and Chokamela from Maharashtra; Basavanna, Purandara Dasa, Akka Mahadevi, Allamma Prabhu and Kanakadas from Karnataka; Tyagaraja, Yogi Vemanna, Annamacharya and Ramadas from Andhra Pradesh; saints such as the sixty-three Nayanars from the Saiva tradition (four of whom—Sundarar, Appar, Sambandar and Manikavachagar—are considered to be especially holy) and the twelve Alwars of Tamil Nadu belonging to the Vaishnava traditions as well as several others. An exhaustive list is not possible. Some include Guru Nanak in this list, although he founded a separate Sikh religion. Nimbarka and Vallabhacharya wrote treatises on devotion though in Sanskrit. Bulle Shah is also named as a Bhakti saint from Punjab though he was a Muslim. The three great philosophers, Sankara, Ramanuja and Madhvacharya are also listed among the Bhakti saints, although they wrote in

Sanskrit and Sankara preached the path of knowledge rather than *bhakti*. Some sages like Trailinga Swami, Sadasiva Brahmendra and Appaya Dikshitar either did not preach or were more philosophical. Consequently, they were not as popular as the other saints of the Bhakti movement.

A few quotes provide a glimpse into the Bhakti movement and why it became so popular. Kabir says

कबिरा जब पैदा हुए जग हँसा हम रोये | ऐसी करनी कर चलो हम हँसे जग रोये ||

Kabira jab paida hue jag hansa hum roye. Aisi karni kar chalo hum hanse jag roye.

[When Kabir was born, the world laughed and I cried. Do such things that when you die, you laugh and the world weeps.]

Referring to the practice of telling beads, Kabir says:

माला फेरत जुग भया, फिरा न मन का फेर, कर का मनका डार दे, मन का मनका फेर |

Mala pherat jug bhaya, phira na man ka pher; kar ka manka dar de, man ka manka pher.

[A long time has gone by in telling the beads, but the confusion in the mind has not gone. Stop rotating the beads with your hands and instead rotate the pearls in your own mind. (There is a play on the word '*manka*' which means 'of the mind' as well as 'pearl'.)]

पाहन पूजे हरि मिले, तो मैं पूजूँ पहार । ताते ये चाकी भली, पीस खाय संसार ||

Paahan Pooje Hari Mile, To Main Poojoon Pahaar.
Taate Ye Chaakee Bhalee, Pees Khaay Sansaar.

[If by worshipping a stone (idol) I can obtain God, I will worship the hill (of stone). Better is the stone grinder whose (wheat) flour the world eats. (He is speaking against idol worship.)]

He gives an Advaitic verse for the common folks in the local language:

साहिब मेरा एक है, दुजः कहा न जाए
दुजः साहिब जो कहूं, साहिब खड़ा रसाई

Saahib mera ek hai, duja kaha na jaaye,
Duja Saahib jo kahun, sahib khada rachaaye.

[My Lord is One without a second. Even if I say there is another Lord, it is the (same) Lord's play or creation.]

Kabir was a seeker of the Formless God. However, most of the saints were devoted to a Personal God. We give three examples of saints devoted to Krishna, the Divine Mother in the form of Kali and Rama. Meera was a devotee of Krishna, a princess who leaves her husband and renounces royal life. Krishna lived thousands of years before Meera. Some of her songs sung even today are:

सांसो की माला पे सिमरूं मैं पि का नाम

Saanson ki mala pe simero main pee ka naam

[In the garland of my breaths, I will remember my Lord's name.]

Again, she says (sort of) addressing the world:

अब किस्मत के हाथ है इस बंधन की लाज; मैंने तो मन लिख दिया साँवरिया के नाम

Ab kismaq ke haath hai is bandhan ki laaj; maine to man likh diya sanwariya ke naam.

[Now the honour (or good name) of this bond (relationship between Krishna and me) is in fate's hands. I have written in my mind my Beloved (Lord's) name.]

The blind saint, Surdas has a personal relation with Krishna. Addressing Krishna, he says:

हाथ छुड़ावत जात हो निर्बल जानके मोहे; हिरदय में से जाओ तब मैं जानु तोहे

Haath chhudavat jaat ho nirbal janke mohe; hriday mein se jao tab janu tohe.

[You leave my hand and go, thinking I am weak. Leave my heart and go, then I will know you.]

Some attribute this verse to Meera and not to Surdas. All these verses show why they became popular with the masses who wanted to have a personal relation with God.

Ramprasad was a devotee of Kali, the Divine Mother. Some of his sayings and songs, originally in Bengali, are given in translated form below. Referring to his own state of mind while worshiping the Mother, he says:

I drink no ordinary wine but the Wine of Everlasting Bliss as I repeat my Mother Kali's name.

Like Meera challenging Krishna, Ramprasad too challenges his Divine Mother:

Mother, am I Thine eight-months child? Thy red eyes cannot frighten me! My riches are Thy Lotus Feet, which Siva holds upon His breast; Yet, when I seek my heritage, I meet with excuses and delays. A deed of gift I hold in my heart, attested by Thy

Husband Siva; I shall sue Thee, if I must, and with a
single point shall win.[1]

Tyagaraja was a devotee of Rama and composed in Telugu.
He wrote several hundreds of songs that are sung in classical
music concerts even today. In one his songs, expressing the
rapture of devotion to Rama, he says:

What greater joy can there be, O Rama?
He concludes with the following words:
Chanting your name makes the worlds effulgent.
In another song, he addresses his own mind and says:
Does wealth give happiness or does Rama give
happiness? (O mind, you decide).

In yet another song, he delves deep into philosophy and,
addressing Rama, says:

For the wise one whose mind is under control, what
need is there of *mantras* (sacred syllables), and *tantras*
(mystic symbols)? For he who knows he is not the body,
what need is there of penance, O son of Dasaratha (i.e.,
Rama)?

Since the songs were composed in regional languages,
they are highly popular in their respective regions but
remain largely unknown outside. However, in a sense, this

does not matter because similar songs are available in all languages. There are literally thousands of them. They are devotional and depict a very human relationship between the devotee and God in language that is easy to understand. They directly address God as master, friend, lover, father, mother or child and sing of an intimate relationship with the Divine. They also express some deeper truths found in the Great Philosophies. The songs and poetry are composed by saints, both men and women, who were regarded as enlightened and came from all sections of society. Their compositions were not only well known back then but have been popular for centuries and continue to be sung even today.

These saints had a tremendous impact on Hinduism. In society, there was an easy acceptance of the idea that God can be worshipped in various ways. A devotee of one God accepts that the same God in another form is worshipped by a devotee of another God or Goddess. The same devotee may pray to various gods.

13

POPULAR HINDUISM

Today, Hinduism permeates day-to-day life in various ways. Like other religions, there are formal places of worship, namely temples. There is perhaps a temple in every village. They may not always be built according to prescribed rules but according to local belief and convenience. Many homes have a shrine where images or idols of one or the god or goddess, sometimes several of them are kept and worshipped daily. Sometimes there are only pictures of some gods and goddesses even in the small dwellings of seasonal migrant labour. Rituals are an important part of religion for many people. This includes bathing, reciting sacred texts or *mantras*, fasting, and celebrating various festivals. Offering *naivedyam* or some food or other gift during worship, and later taking it as *prasad* or blessing from God is common. Various important aspects of life like marriage and funerals are regarded as religious occasions and sacred texts and *mantras* are chanted. There is also a set of beliefs specific to each God about auspicious days of worship, fasting and so on. Fasting of some sort on days like *ekadasi* (the eleventh day after full moon or new moon) is a fairly common practice among some people. Rituals done in the right spirit help many people to focus the mind and keep it on God. Astrology is invoked to calculate auspicious times for starting some work and avoiding inauspicious dates and times. Going regularly on pilgrimage to sacred temples and places is also common.

However, you also find a significant number of people who by temperament are not inclined to rituals. This is also accepted. A few are more rational and do not believe in God or are agnostic. But for social and cultural reasons some of them may follow some of the rituals or practices. Some may refuse to do even that. All this is accepted without any social ostracization. In the same family you find some worshipping different gods, those who do not believe in God, and those who accept one philosophy or the other. There is a sense of acceptance of different points of view without giving up one's own.

Apart from all this there is something that can be described as folk religion. Mainstream religion and folk religion have influenced each other over the centuries. Thus, the religious practices of various tribal communities and those of so-called low castes who were excluded are also very much present. Rituals, worship and deities are different. For instance, until recently, smallpox and other dreaded diseases were thought to come from a goddess.

By appeasing her one could get relief. Harvests, marriage, funerals and other events are observed by invoking some local deity.

Caste is another reality in India. There are various views about it. Some reject it, others justify it. Some reject Hinduism because of caste discrimination. Some say originally caste was *jati* and determined by individual aptitude and temperament, not by birth. Confining privileges to one group based on birth was a distortion. This led to a kind of calcification into caste over time. Still others say it is not a part of Hinduism, but simply a social practice. If it serves no purpose, it should be done away with.

The spiritual texts such as the Upanishads, the Brahma Sutras, the Six Darsanas and the later philosophies do not refer to caste at all. There are stray references in the Vedas to caste, for instance, in the Purusha Suktam. The Smritis like the Manu Smriti refer to caste and its different roles. The Bhagavad Gita has a passing reference to caste. Others point to several revered sages and the *avatars* who were not Brahmins. Veda Vyasa, whose birth is observed today as Guru Purnima by all castes alike, was a son born out of wedlock to the fisherwoman Satyavati and the sage Parashara. Rama and Krishna, worshipped as *avatars*, were Kshatriyas and not Brahmins. The Gayatri Mantra in the Rig Veda, given to young boys at the *upananaya* ceremony, is attributed to the sage Viswamitra who was not born as a Brahmin. This *mantra* and the ceremony are given in practice largely to unmarried Brahmin boys in a special ceremony. Through rigorous *tapas*, Viswamitra became a *brahmarishi*. The Chandogya Upanishad is one of the most highly revered of the ten Principal Upanishads. The teaching is given to Satyakama Jabala, a young boy whose mother tells him she does not know who his father was. Thus, some point to the fact that caste as it was originally understood was not determined by birth but by temperament or achievement. In such a voluminous literature, there is a justification for nearly all points of view, just like we find in the various philosophies.

A few things are perhaps unique to popular Hinduism. One is the idea that God exists in innumerable forms. As a corollary, all ways of worshipping that God are accepted. The same individual goes to various temples dedicated to different gods and goddesses. This often manifests in a peculiar way—orthodox or conservative in one's personal life, but liberal in accepting those following other ways. At a personal level there are no watertight compartments between devotion to various gods, between devotion and knowledge, the formless God and God with form and so on. Another idea is the immanent divinity of all living beings, that is, the idea that the Atman resides in all of us. It is also accepted that it is possible to realize this even today. The reverence shown to those regarded as enlightened irrespective of their gender or caste is something that has to be seen to be understood. This extends to saints and sages of the past, those from other religions, beliefs and ways of worship, and to those still alive. Vivekananda says that even the king or political leader stands up on receiving a *sannyasi*. In a real sense, the highest regard in popular Hinduism is reserved for men and women of God.

CONCLUSIONS

Some Common Bases

All branches of Hinduism accept the primacy of the Vedas and the Upanishads. Among the various ideas and philosophies in Hinduism, there are some essentials that are common. One is the idea that the highest God is formless and is the Supreme Reality, Brahman. Another is the idea that there is a divine spark or Atman in every living being. All agree that Brahman is of the nature of Consciousness and Bliss. Differences exist about what Brahman is and Its relationship with the Atman. According to Advaita philosophy, Brahman is the only reality and the world and the living beings are perceived due to false perception or ignorance. This is called *maya*, the inexpressible principle that leads to the false perception of the unreal or temporary world as real. Anything that has form and attributes is limited. Therefore, Brahman is formless and without any attributes. Knowledge establishes that it was always

Brahman and *maya* disappears. The Atman is the same as Brahman. Another view of Visishtadvaita is that Brahman is qualified by the world and the living beings and pervades it. Brahman has attributes, and the world is real and not unreal or *maya*. The Atman is essentially the same as Brahman but is separate from it. Dvaita a third philosophy says that Brahman is different from the world and the living beings. The individual soul is not essentially the same as Brahman but is a reflection of it. Down the ages there have been debates about *nirguna* Brahman without any attributes and *saguna* Brahman with attributes. However, there is no dispute about the existence of Brahman that confers bliss, is of the nature of Consciousness and which leads to liberation.

These different points of view are sought to be reconciled by the well-known saying:

देहबुद्ध्या तु दासोऽस्मि जीवबुद्ध्या त्वदंशकः |
आत्मबुद्ध्या त्वमेवाहमिति मे निश्चिता मतिः ||

Deha-Buddhyaa Tu Dasosmi Jiva-Buddhyaa Tvad-Anshakah |
Aatma-Buddhyaa Tvam-Evaaham Iti Me Nishchita Matih ||

[When I identify myself with the body, I am your servant, O Lord. When I identify with the individual soul, I am a part of you. When I identify with the *Atman*, I am identical to you.˙]

Identification with the body leads to Dvaita, identification with one's individuality leads to Visishtadvaita, and identification with the Atman leads to Advaita. It also gives a hint that the same individual can experience all three 'philosophies' at different points of time.

Vivekananda observed, 'What Ramakrishna Paramahamsa and I have done is to show that the many and the One are the same reality seen by the same mind at different times and different attitudes.'[1]

What, then, of the various gods and goddesses? All agree that they emerge from the same Brahman. Even Advaita says that in the realm of empirical experience, such gods do exist but are emanations or projections of Brahman.

Another common belief is that of liberation or freedom from the cycle of birth and death called *moksha, mukti, nirvana* or *kaivalya*. This is not merely an unconscious merging into the Infinite, but is also the source of bliss and knowledge. The individual *jiva* is what attains liberation. The nature of liberation is described differently by the different schools of philosophy. According to Advaita, the liberated *jiva* becomes one with Brahman and is never again

---

˙ In Christianity, 'Our Father, who art in heaven' is Dvaita, 'I am the vine, you are the branches' is similar to Visishtadvaita, and 'My Father and I are one' is similar to the Advaita.

reborn. According to Visishtadvaita, the *jiva* is freed from rebirth but is permanently in Vaikuntha, enjoys eternal bliss but remains separate from Brahman (who is a Personal God with attributes) though in essence the same. According to Dvaita, the liberated *jiva* attains bliss but the degree of bliss is according to what it has earned. The liberated *jiva* is not identical to Vishnu, but a reflection of Him. All philosophies except Dvaita accept that eventually everyone is liberated even if takes several births to achieve such liberation.

Since there is a concept of liberation, another common belief is in *karma* and rebirth. These ideas are common to other Indian religions including Jainism, Buddhism and Sikhism.* Ignorance, attachment or unfulfilled desire leads the *jiva* to seek rebirth. Human birth is usually considered to be a prerequisite for attaining liberation. The *jiva* has an opportunity to attain liberation. After several lifetimes of experience, the individual *jiva* begins to wonder what this is all about, seeks something else and starts working its way to liberation.

A belief unique to Hinduism is the concept of the *avatar* or incarnation of God, of which there are many, and perhaps more to come in the future.† Devotion to

---

* The Bible has a reference to John the Baptist, who was a reincarnation of Elijah, a more ancient prophet.
† This is analogous to science where there are many scientists. Revelation and the descent of God as *avatar* is also not limited to a few individuals.

the *avatar* of one's choice and following their teachings is a valid and legitimate part of Hinduism. However, this is not insisted upon, giving freedom to the individual to chart their own path.

While it is not stated clearly in the texts, it is widely accepted that making progress in religious life, particularly in one's spiritual journey, is helped by a teacher or *guru* who is enlightened. Implicit is the belief that enlightenment is possible for anyone.

Summary

There are so many sacred texts that it is impossible to cover all of them in such a short introductory text. They include the entire range of subjects and themes, from revealed texts to metaphysics and philosophy based on logic, various practices and rituals that help to make our life better in the here and now and also to reach the goal of life. There are also texts on secular subjects such as grammar, medicine, arts, music as well as astrology. The texts are in prose, poetry, hymns and aphorisms (*sutras*). Theories about the origin of the universe, cosmic cycles, stories of gods, human stories, epics, legends and myths are also part of this vast literature.

The Vedas, including the Upanishads, are the revealed texts—the Shruti. The Brahma Sutras provide a systematic basis for the revealed texts. The *darsanas* are philosophies that explain the nature of reality, God, human beings, the universe and the relationship between them. The Bhagavad Gita is a unique text that is preached by the *avatar* Krishna and is a part of the foundation of Hinduism. The Vedas, the Brahma Sutras and the Bhagavad Gita are known as the *prasthana traya*, the three most sacred texts. The later Smritis lay down guidelines of *dharma*, the proper way of living. The Puranas introduce various personal gods and goddesses, myths, legends and heroes and give a popular touch to religion while also giving some deep spiritual truths. The Agama Sastras are more esoteric and use *mantras*, rituals and symbols for progressing on the spiritual path. The Itihasas, that is, the Ramayana and the Mahabharata, are epic poems about historical events with interesting stories and religious, moral and ethical teachings. The epics are based on two of the *avatars*, Rama and Krishna. The later philosophies explain the aphorisms of the Brahma Sutras and the Upanishads in more detail and give different doctrines about the nature of reality, God, living beings and the universe. Practical methods of reaching the goal of life are scattered across the various texts. Some of these methods are handed down from teacher to disciple.

Each of the texts—the Vedas, Upanishads, Brahma Sutras, Bhagavad Gita, the Puranas, Smritis, Agama Sastras, the six earliest *darsanas* as well as the later philosophies—require long study. In addition, there are other texts that are not classified in an orthodox manner but are nevertheless considered sacred, such as the various Gitas as well as texts like the Tripura Rahasya, Adhyatma Ramayana and Yoga Vasishtha. They explain the Vedantic truths by using dialogue, stories, poetry and simple language. It is unlikely that any one individual has read and studied all the sacred texts.

Various methods are given for knowing that Truth, including knowledge (*jnana*), devotion (*bhakti*), selfless work (Karma Yoga), control of the mind (Raja Yoga based on meditation). Some interpret these methods as suitable for various aspects of our personality. *Jnana* uses the faculty of thinking, *bhakti* appeals to our faculty of feeling, Karma Yoga to the ability to act and work, and Yoga or meditation to willing or will power. Perhaps the great insight was that by giving a higher turn to these faculties we can gain the highest purpose of life.

It is also accepted that not everyone is interested in liberation. Various rituals are prescribed, including some elaborate ones that require days to perform while following certain personal disciplines. However, these are not in the form of dos and don'ts. It is for the individual to choose. All kinds of attitudes are accepted from those who worship God for personal well-being, for solace when in distress, for prosperity, good health, wealth, family and so on, to those seeking religious merit, or those seeking liberation. Hinduism says God accepts everyone and responds according to the attitude of the devotee. Those who do not worship any Personal God but seek Truth or peace or liberation are also accepted. Atheists and agnostics are accepted. People of other religions are not condemned either.* In the typical Hindu way of thinking, sages and wise men are all respected and revered.

The concept of God is left to the individual. God could be the *nirguna*, *nirakara*, attribute-less, formless Brahman, God with attributes but without form, God with both attributes and form, or any of the various gods and goddesses that are worshipped. In recent times, Sri Ramakrishna pointed out how these apparently contradictory ideas about God could be reconciled. He said that in the North Pole the ice never melts. In the same way the Formless takes a form in response to the love of the devotees. When the Sun of Knowledge rises, the ice melts and everything become formless. But both the formless and forms come from the same reality.

Hinduism does not have one philosophy or one teaching. There is no one founder. It may seem bewildering to someone who sees it for the first time. However, perhaps recognizing human nature and its diversity, Hinduism

---

* Many Hindus visit places of worship of other religions, sometimes in large numbers. It is respect for the saint, the sage, the wise person that draws them, not the religion. This acceptance perhaps comes from the very nature of Hinduism with so many gods, goddesses, sages, *rishis* and philosophies.

recognized long ago that different ways and paths are needed for different individuals. One size does not fit all. Hinduism does not condemn even atheists or sinners to go to eternal hell. It continues to offer hope to people of all faiths. The Vedas, the most ancient and most sacred of its texts, declare that merely knowing the Vedas is not enough. It even goes on to say that belief in the Vedas is not essential for human life. Any path followed with sincerity will lead to the same goal. Two famous sayings of the Rig Veda embody the spirit of enquiry into Truth that lies at the heart of Hinduism and may be relevant even today:

> *Ekam sat, vipra bahuda vadanti* [Truth is One, sages call it by various names]
> *Aa no bhadrah kratvo yantu visvatah'* [Let noble thoughts come to us from every side]

The same Truth can be reached in various ways, and all noble ideas that help us to reach that goal are welcome.

GLOSSARY

Atman	the Self in every living being which is Conscious and Divine
Agama	scriptures that deal with ritual, construction of temples, *yantras* or symbols and so on
Ahamkara	ego
Brahman	root: vast, expansive, all-pervasive. Refers to the Ultimate Reality that is of the nature of Existence, Knowledge and Bliss
Chit	consciousness or knowledge
Chitta	the storehouse of mental impressions, often translated as 'mind-stuff'
darsana	literally, 'to see'; refers to philosophical systems as well
Deva	literally, 'the Shining One', refers to various deities, especially in the Vedas
dharma	that which supports; religion, code of conduct, duties
guna	quality; *sattva guna* is calm, *rajas* is active and energetic, *tamas* is dullness
guru	the teacher; literally, 'one who removes darkness or ignorance'

Glossary

Ishwara	Isa or Lord, and *vara* supreme. Refers to the Supreme Lord
japa	utterance of a sacred set of syllables or *mantra*
jnana	knowledge. Can refer to knowledge derived from the senses, by reason, intuition or spiritual revelation
karma	action; refers to Vedic ritual as well as action and the impact of action on the mind
mantra	a word-sound or incantation; that which protects the mind
maya	illusion
Nirakara	without form; *nirakara Brahman* means 'the Ultimate Reality without form'
Nirguna	without attributes; *nirguna Brahman* means 'the Ultimate Reality without attributes'
Om	mystic syllable; refers to the entire universe and the entirety of time and yet which is beyond both; it is also a *mantra*
Purusha	the Consciousness or awareness within all; it is also called 'Atman'
sabda	word; it usually refers to sacred verses from the scriptures
sadhana	means for accomplishing something; it also refers to the accomplishment itself
Sakara	with form
Saguna	with attributes; *saguna Brahman* means 'the Ultimate Reality with attributes'
Samadhi	enlightenment, super-consciousness; final state reached by meditation
Sanatana	eternal; Sanatana Dharma literally means 'the Eternal Religion', now known as Hinduism

sannyasa	renunciation. A *sannyasi* is a monk while a *sannyasini* is a nun
sastra	scripture
Siddhanta	a doctrine or philosophy
sutra	a short, terse aphorism that often expresses a deep thought
Upanishad	scriptures found at the end of the Vedas; said to be the Revealed Texts
Veda	the earliest sacred texts; there are four—Rig, Yajur, Sama and Atharva Vedas—and they also contain the Upanishads
Vedanta	literally, 'the end or goal of the Vedas'; the Upanishads collectively comprise the Vedanta. The system of philosophy based on the Vedanta Sutras is also called Vedanta
Vidya	knowledge
Yoga	derived from '*yuj*', meaning 'to yoke or join'; refers to the union of the individual soul with the Divine

NOTES

Chapter 1: The Vedas

1. The *rishi* or seer is also called a *'mantra drashta'* or 'the one who "sees" the sacred *mantras'*. Here, both the act of hearing, as in *'shruti'*, and of seeing, as in *'mantra drashta'*, refer to revelation. A well-known reference is that of Moses who saw a burning bush and heard the voice of God. Although the Old Testament refers to 'seeing' and 'hearing', it is understood to be a revelation.

2. Buddhism and Jainism did not accept the final authority of the Vedas. Though these great religions are from India, they are not part of orthodox Hinduism, which usually classifies them as *'naastika'* (literally, 'that which does not accept the Vedas'). In the Bhagavad Gita, there are references to the ritual portion of the Vedas or the Karma Kanda. The Gita says that those who follow the Karma Kanda will reap the fruits of that *karma*, enjoying them in this life and in the afterlife, and then be born again. But those who follow the Gita's teachings will go beyond that and get final liberation. However, even the Gita does not say that following the Vedic rituals is useless.

3. Swami Vivekananda, 'Vedanta in Its Application to Indian Life', in *Complete Works*, Vol. 3, available at https://www.ramakrishnavivekananda.info/vivekananda/volume_3/lectures_from_colombo_to_almora/vedanta_in_its_applications_to_indian_life.htm.

4. The Quran has less than 7,000 verses. The Old Testament has over 23,000 verses while the New Testament has about 7,500 verses. There is no exact information about the length of the Buddhist scriptures based on the different versions of Buddhism. However, if we look at all the Hindu scriptures in their entirety, they are far lengthier. For instance, taken together, the Puranas have at least 400,000 verses. Besides, there are other texts such as the Smritis, the Vedangas, the Itihasas, the Agama Sastras and the Six Darsanas. The Guru Granth Sahib of the Sikh religion has nearly 6000 verses.

5. In different traditions, many experience listening to the recitation or chanting of scriptures as calming, soothing and even healing. Contemporary medical research that measures bodily, nervous and brain conditions corroborates this. See, for instance, Norman Doidge's *The Brain That Changes Itself* (first published by Viking Penguin, USA, 2007). Doidge is a qualified medical doctor who documents the healing impact of Gregorian chants, usually sung by Catholics. There is a similar belief regarding the Quran, and those who chant and listen to its verses have reported similar experiences. The Vedic chants in this sense of healing and soothing the body and mind are very similar.

6. In modern times, the well-known mathematical genius Srinivas Ramanujan often said that mathematical theorems were revealed to him by the Goddess Namagiri. By ancient Vedic interpretation, the mathematical facts have always

existed and Ramanujan merely discovered them through hard work (*tapas*) and intuition. According to modern psychology, his faith made him believe that the mathematical truths he obtained by intuition, hard work and thinking came from the Goddess. Traditional belief, still prevalent today, would nonetheless say that such truths were indeed revealed by Goddess Namagiri. Note that Ramanujan continued to work very hard at mathematics almost till his death in spite of his belief in the Goddess. As eminent non-Hindu mathematicians have noted the theorems of Ramanujan were correct.

7. Swami Vivekananda, 'The Essence of Religion', in *Complete Works*, Vol. 8, available at https://www.ramakrishnavivekananda. info/vivekananda/volume_8/notes_of_class_talks_and_ lectures/the_essence_of_religion.htm.

8. The Brihadaranyaka Upanishad (2.4.10) says that the Vedas are God's (Ishwara's) breath or '*nishwasitam*'.

9. Sri Chandrasekharendra Saraswati, *The Vedas* (Mumbai: Bharatiya Vidya Bhavan, 1998), 49.

10. Swami Vivekananda, 'Sayings and Utterances', in *Complete Works*, Vol. 5, available at https://www.ramakrishnavivekananda. info/vivekananda/volume_5/sayings_and_utterances.htm.

11. There are later Puranic legends about the twofold Yajur Veda. However, there is no reference to this in the Vedas themselves. According to one legend, the Krishna Yajur Veda was first revealed to the sage Yajnavalkya by his *guru*, Vaishampayana. Due to some dispute, the *guru* asked his disciple to return the Veda. The disciple accepted the validity of the *guru*'s instruction and returned it. The original version is known as the Krishna Yajur Veda. Yajnavalkya then involved the Sun God who revealed the Shukla Yajur Veda.

12. A discussion of the *mantra* can be found at http://sanskrit.org/gayatri-mantra/.

13. Gospel of Sri Ramakrishna, available at http://www.ramakrishnavivekananda.info/gospel/gospel.htm.

14. 'According to the theories of physics, if we were to look at the Universe one second after the Big Bang, what we would see is a 10-billion degree sea of neutrons, protons, electrons, anti-electrons (positrons), photons, and neutrinos. Then, as time went on, we would see the Universe cool, the neutrons either decaying into protons and electrons or combining with protons to make deuterium (an isotope of hydrogen). As it continued to cool, it would eventually reach the temperature where electrons combined with nuclei to form neutral atoms. Before this "recombination" occurred, the Universe would have been opaque because the free electrons would have caused light (photons) to scatter the way sunlight scatters from the water droplets in clouds. But when the free electrons were absorbed to form neutral atoms, the Universe suddenly became transparent. Those same photons—the afterglow of the Big Bang known as cosmic background radiation—can be observed today.' See https://science.nasa.gov/astrophysics/focus-areas/what-powered-the-big-bang. Perhaps the word '*salilam*' in the Nasadiya Suktam refers to some primordial substance, which we translate as 'water', and 'mist' in English.

Chapter 2: Upanishads or Vedanta

1. A well-known example from outside India is Moses who saw the burning bush (that did not burn) and heard the voice of God.

2.   Swami Paramananda, Kena Upanishad, available at https://
     www.hinduwebsite.com/sacredscripts/hinduism/parama/
     kena.asp.
3.   Tejobindu Upanishad, Chapter 3, Krishna Yajur Veda.
4.   Taittirya Upanishad, Krishna Yajur Veda.
5.   Swami Vivekananda, 'Vedic Religious Ideals', in *Complete Works*,
     Vol. 1, available at https://www.ramakrishnavivekananda.
     info/vivekananda/volume_1/lectures_and_discourses/vedic_
     religious_ideals.htm.
6.   Swami Vivekananda, 'God in Everything', in *Complete Works*,
     Vol. 2, available at https://www.ramakrishnavivekananda.info/
     vivekananda/volume_2/jnana-yoga/god_in_everything.htm.
7.   References to sound 'Om': Mandukya Upanishad, '*Om-ityedat
     aksharam idam sarvam*' or Om is the Imperishable and is all
     this. Taittirya Upanishad, '*Om iti Brahma. Om itidam sarvam*'
     or 'Om is Brahman'. Om is all this. Katha Upanishad, '*Etadyeva
     aksharam Brahma . . .*' or 'This Imperishable Om is Brahma.'
     Prasna Upanishad, '*Etadvay Satyakama param cha aparam cha
     Brahma yad-Omkara*' or 'This O Satyakama, is the lower and
     higher Brahman and is Om.' Mundaka Upanishad, '*Om ityeva
     dhayat Atmanam*' or 'Meditate on the Atman or Self with the
     help of Om.' Maitri Upanishad, '*Om ityevam dhyayata*' or
     'Meditate on the Self as Om.' Chandogya Upanishad, '*Om
     indeed is all these.*'
8.   References to Light: Isa Upanishad, '*Hiranmayena patrena
     satyastapihitam mukham*', or 'In the Golden Vessel is the face
     of Truth'. Also '*rasmin samuha teja*' or 'rays of bright Light'.
     Mundaka Upanishad, '*hiranmaye pare koshe*', 'beyond the
     golden sheath', and '*jyotisham jyoti*', the 'Light of lights'. Also,
     '*Avih sanihitam guhacharam nama*', 'it is effulgent and in the
     Heart', and '*Tad divyam achintya rupam*', 'That (Brahman)

self-effulgent and beyond thought'. Prasna Upanishad, '*sahasra rasmi*', 'the thousand rays'. Also '*jyotir ekam*', 'the one Light'. Taittirya Upanishad, '*Amrito hiranmaya*', 'That Immortality is effulgent'.

9. References to Atman in the Heart: Mundaka Upanishad, '*Antah sarire jyotirmayo hi subhro*', '(It is) in the body, that Light that is pure'. Prasna Upanishad, '*hrdi esha Atma*', 'this Atman resides in the Heart'. Also, '*Ihaiva antah sarire Soumya sa Purusha*', 'here in this body O Soumya, is this Purusha'. Taittirya Upanishad, '*sa ya esha antar hridaya aakasha*', 'That (Atman) is in the Heart space'. Katha Upanishad, '*Atma asya jantor nihito guhayam*', 'The Atman resides in the Heart of all beings'. Also, '*Angushtha matra purusho Madhya Atmani tishthati*' and '*Angushtha matra Purusho Antar Atma*', 'of the size of a thumb, in the body resides that Atman, in the Heart'. Aitareya Upanishad says, 'Etam eva Purusham Brahma, tatamama pasyat', 'this very Purusha he saw as Brahman'.

10. References to bliss: Taittiriya Upanishad, '*etam anadamaya Atma*', 'that blissful Self'; '*Anandam Brahmano vidvan*', 'he who knows the Bliss of Brahman'; '*Anandam Brahmeti vyajana*t', 'he knew the Bliss of Brahman'. Brihadaranyaka Upanishad, '*Etasyaiva-anandasya-anyani bhutani matram upajivanti*', 'This is that Supreme Bliss. On a particle of this Bliss the beings live'. Mundaka Upanishad says, '*Ananda rupam amritam yad vibhati*', 'That (Self or Atman or Brahman) shines as Bliss'.

11. References to meditation: Mundaka Upanishad, '*pasyate nishkalam dhyaya mana*', 'see the Indivisible through meditation'. Again, '*eshah anuh Atma chetasa veditavyo*', 'This subtle Self is to be known through the pure mind or

Consciousness'. Also, '*Om ityeva dhyayatha Atmanam*', 'meditate on the Atman or Self through Om alone'. Katha Upanishad, '*Etadhyeva aksharam jnatva yo yadichhati tasya Tat*', 'this Om imperishable when known (through meditation) gives That (Brahman) to the aspirant'.

12. Will Durant, *The Complete Story of Civilization*, Vol. 1 (New York: Simon & Schuster, 2014).

Chapter 3: Important Concepts in Hinduism

1. Swami Vivekananda, 'Questions and Answers', in *Complete Works*, Vol. 5, available at https://www.ramakrishnavivekananda. info/vivekananda/volume_5/questions_and_answers/ questions_and_answers_contents.htm.

2. Lecture on Gita, in Swami Vivekananda, *Complete Works*, Vol. 1, available at https://www.ramakrishnavivekananda.info/ vivekananda/complete_works.htm.

3. Swami Vivekananda, 'Buddha's Message to the World', in *Complete Works*, Vol. 8, available at https://www. ramakrishnavivekananda.info/vivekananda/volume_8/ lectures_and_discourses/buddhas_message.htm.

4. Swami Vivekananda, 'Christ, the Messenger', in *Complete Works*, Vol. 4, available at https://www.ramakrishnavivekananda. info/vivekananda/volume_4/lectures_and_discourses/christ_ the_messenger.htm.

5. Ibid.

6. The idea of giving up possessions is clearly present in many religions. Buddhism gave rise to the earliest organized monastic order. *Munis* and *sannyasis* in the Vedic times did not, however, belong to any organized order. In the New Testament, Jesus Christ observes, 'Foxes have holes and birds have nests, but

the Son of Man has no place to lay his head' and 'It is easier for a camel to pass through the eye of a needle than a rich man to enter the gates of Heaven'. Christ also says, 'If you want to be perfect, go, sell your possessions and give to the poor, and you will have treasure in heaven. Then come, follow Me' and 'Behold the fowls of the air: for they sow not, neither do they reap, nor gather into barns; yet your heavenly Father feedeth them. Are ye not much better than they?' The Quran says that 'All wealth belongs to Allah.'

7. Sri Chandrasekharendra Saraswati, *The Vedas* (Mumbai: Bharatiya Vidya Bhavan, 1998).

Chapter 4: The Six Darsanas or Philosophies

1. The *jnanendriyas* are the ear (*srotra*), eye (*chakshu*), tongue (*jivha*), skin (*tvak*) and nose (*ghrana*). The *karmendriyas* are the organs of speech (*vak*), hands (*pani*), feet (*pada*), excretion (*payu*, anus) and reproduction (*upasthah*). The five *panchabhutas* are *akasa* (space), *vayu* (air), *agni* (fire), *jal* or *aapa* (water), and *prithvi* or *bhoomi* (earth). The five *tanmatras* are *sabda* (sound), *rupa* (form), *rasana* (taste), *sparsha* (touch) and *gandha* (smell).

Chapter 5: The Brahma Sutras

1. Swami Vireswarananda, *Brahma Sutras* (Advaita Ashram, 1936). Gives a translation of Madhavacharya's Sanskrit quote from the Padma Purana, an ancient Hindu text. Madhavacharya was the author of the Dvaita philosophy, to be discussed in a later chapter.

Chapter 7: Puranas

1. Ganesh Swaminathan, *From the Beginning of Time: Modern Science and the Puranic Universe* (Chennai: Notion Press, 2020); Sidharth Chhabra and Madhavendra Puri Das, *The Big Bang and the Sages: Modern Science Catches Up with the Ancient Purāṇas* (Chennai: Notion Press, 2020).

Chapter 8: Agama Sastras

1. T.M.P. Mahadevan, *Outlines of Hinduism* (Mumbai: Chetana, 1999).
2. Swami Lokeswarananda, ed., *Studies on the Tantras* (Kolkata: Ramakrishna Mission Institute of Culture, 1997).

Chapter 11: The Great Philosophies

1. Swami Vireswarananda, *Brahma Sutras* (Mayavati, Almora: Advaita Ashrama, 1936).
2. Swami Vivekananda, 'Fundamentals of Religion', in *Complete Works*, Vol. 4.

Chapter 12: The Bhakti Tradition

1. See https://www.ramakrishnavivekananda.info/gospel/gospel.htm.

Conclusions

1. See https://www.ramakrishnavivekananda.info/vivekananda/complete_works.htm.